A LITTLE GIANT® BOOK

WORD SEARCHES

MARK DANNA

STERLING

New York / London
www.sterlingpublishing.com/kids

STERLING and the distinctive Sterling logo
are registered trademarks of Sterling Publishing Co., Inc.

Lot#:

6   8   10   9   7

08/12

Published by Sterling Publishing Co., Inc.
387 Park Avenue South, New York, NY 10016
© 2008 by Mark Danna
Materials compiled from the following Mark Danna books:
Clever Word Search Puzzles for Kids, © 2004;
Fantastic Word Search Puzzles for Kids, © 2004;
and *Baffling Word Search Puzzles for Kids*, © 2005.
Distributed in Canada by Sterling Publishing
C/o Canadian Manda Group, 165 Dufferin Street
Toronto, Ontario, Canada M6K 3H6
Distributed in the United Kingdom by GMC Distribution Services
Castle Place, 166 High Street, Lewes, East Sussex, England BN7 1XU
Distributed in Australia by Capricorn Link (Australia) Pty. Ltd.
P.O. Box 704, Windsor, NSW 2756, Australia

Printed in China
All rights reserved

Sterling ISBN-13: 978-1-4027-4667-3
ISBN-10: 1-4027-4667-9

For information about custom editions, special sales, premium and
corporate purchases, please contact Sterling Special Sales
Department at 800-805-5489 or specialsales@sterlingpublishing.com.

Introduction

What's a word search puzzle?

A word search puzzle is a game of hide-and-seek: we hide the words; you go seek them. Each puzzle has two main parts: a grid and a word list. The grid looks like a meaningless jumble of letters, but it actually hides all the words and phrases in the word list. Most word search girds are square or rectangular, but each grid in this book comes in a distinctive picture shape that relates to the theme of the puzzle.

Words and phrases always go in a straight line— horizontally, vertically, or diagonally. Horizontal words go straight across to the right or backward to the left. Vertical words go straight down or straight up. Diagonal words slant from left-to-right or right-to-left and go either upward or downward along the angle. So words can go in eight possible directions—along the lines of a plus sign (+) or a multiplication sign (x).

What else should I know?

In the grid, the same letter may be used in more than one word. This happens when words cross each other from two or more directions. You'll see lots of shared letters in this book because we've made sure that every word in a grid crosses at least one other word, and that all the words in a grid interconnect. It's a nice touch that's often missing elsewhere.

When you look for words and phrases in the grid, ignore all punctuation and spacing in the word list. For example, the phrase "NOBODY'S HOME!" in the word list would appear in the grid, in some direction, as NOBODYSHOME. Also, ignore all words in brackets like [THE] and [A]. These have been added at times to make certain word list choices more understandable, but they will not appear in the grid.

How do I get started?

Some people look for across words first. Others begin with the long words or ones with less common letters like Q, Z, X, or J. Still others start at the top of the list and work their way in order straight down to the bottom. Try a few ways and see what works best for you.

How do I mark the hidden words?

Loop them, draw a line straight through them, or circle each individual letter. Whatever you choose, cross the words off the word list as you find them in the grid so as to avoid confusion. And be sure to be neat.

What's in this book?

There are 137 puzzles, each with a different shape and theme. Word lists generally have 20 to 25 items. With a few exceptions, the puzzles are all about the same difficulty level, so feel free to jump around and do the puzzles in any order you like. As a bonus, every puzzle contains a hidden message! After you've circled all the words and phrases in the grid, read all the uncircled letters from left to right, top to bottom, to spell out the answer to a "punny" riddle, a punch line to a silly joke, or words connected to the theme. When you try to uncover the hidden message, the letters will be in order, but you'll need to figure out how to break them into words and where to add punctuation. That makes this puzzle-within-a-puzzle a real challenge and adds a level of difficulty not usually associated with word search puzzles. If you find it too hard, that's okay. You can still get your laughs by reading the messages in the answer section.

Any final words?

The puzzle titles are playful, so don't be surprised if you're fooled at first as to what the puzzle theme is. And be prepared for a lot of good, silly fun in the hidden messages. Finally, have a great time from start to finish.

1. THAT'S FANTASTIC!

Shaped like the head of a unicorn, the grid contains fantastic creatures from myth and the movies. The hidden message answers the riddle "What did Dracula's frustrated wife say to her husband?"

ALIEN	MERMAID
CYCLOPS	MINOTAUR
DRAGON	OGRE
ELVES	PEGASUS
GENIE	PIXIE
GODZILLA	SEA SERPENT
GREMLIN	[THE] TERMINATOR
HARPY	TROLL
KING KONG	UNICORN
MEDUSA	WOLF MAN

```
                                              N
                                           R
                 G                  O
           Y  O  O  U            C        I
           M  E  D  U  S  A         I
        R  E  Z  D  P  S  D  N
        R  M  I  N  O  T  A  U  R  I
  S  V  L  A  L  I  E  N  N  S  A
  E  L  I  C  Y  P  R  A  H  N  A  G  G
  A  R  Y  M  E  R  M  A  I  D  M  G  O  E
  S  C  G  A  B  F  I        P  I  X  I  E  N
  E  T  R  O  L  L  N           S  O     L  P
  R  U  T  O  E  E  A              L  Y
  P  B  W  A  T  I  T
  E  L  V  E  S  N  O  T
  N  N  I  L  M  E  R  G  Y
  T  G  N  O  K  G  N  I  K
```

2. BE A GOOD SPORT

Shaped like an in-line skate, the grid contains things found in a sporting goods store. The hidden message answers the riddle "Why does the girl listen to pop music when she goes in-line skating?"

BATS	MITT
CLEATS	OARS
CROQUET SET	PUCK
CUE STICK	SKATES
DARTS	SKIS
FLY ROD	SNEAKERS
FOOTBALL	SNORKEL
FRISBEE	SWEATS
JERSEY	TEES
KAYAK	TENT
KNEE PADS	TREADMILL
MATS	WET SUIT

```
    T  B  S  E
 F  C  N  W  A
 R  O  T  E  E  S
 I  U  O  A  T  K
 S  B  A  T  S  A
 B  T  I  S  B  Y
 E  M  R  O  S  A
 E  C  A  A  S  K  L
 T  R  E  A  D  M  I  L  L
 S  O  S  K  A  T  E  S  E  L
 S  Q  H  P  I  S  D  A  P  E  E  N  K
 Y  U  C  U  E  S  T  I  C  K  E  C  S
    E  S  C        D  O  R  Y  L  F
    T  S  K              O  M  E
 A  E  S     R  R  O     C  K  N     A  N  R
 W  O  E  S  N  E  A  K  E  R  S     L  T  T  L
 E  R  T     B  L  J     A  D  E        S  R  S
```

3. WHIRLED VIEW

Shaped like a globe, the grid contains places and things found on a globe. The hidden message answers the riddle "What do you call a globe that's well-known to everyone in every country?"

AFRICA	INDIA
AMAZON	ISLANDS
AMERICAS	LAKES
ANTARCTICA	LAOS
ASIA	[LINES OF] LATITUDE
AUSTRALIA	[LINES OF] LONGITUDE
BAYS	MALI
BORDERS	MOUNTAINS
CITIES	NILE
COUNTRIES	OCEANS
DESERTS	PARIS
EQUATOR	ROME
EUROPE	SEAS
FIJI	TOGO
GULFS	TUNISIA

```
                        A
              E  A  E  S     N     S
         W  E  D  Q  M  Y  T  O              I
      A  M  O  U  N  T  A  I  N  S        A
      O  U  A  T  R  R  B  Z  T  L        M
   R  D  T  S  I  C  E  U  R  O  P  E     E
   C  O  U  N  T  R  I  E  S  F  N  P     R
   R  O  A  I  A  R  S  T  S  E  A  S     I
   A  S  C  I  L  E  A  C  I  R  F  A     C
      A  F  E  D  M  A  L  I  E  I        A
      I  S  L  A  N  D  S  I  J  S        S
         A  T  U  N  I  S  I  A        E
      O           M  G  S  F              K
   S                             A
      E  D  U  T  I  G  N  O  L
               O  I
               O  L  G  U
            S  R  E  D  R  O  B  S
```

4. UP A TREE

Shaped like a Christmas tree ornament, the grid contains things that may be found on or in a tree. The hidden message answers the riddle "What classes did the tree surgeon take in school?"

APPLES	LEAF
BARK	NEST
BATS	NUTS
BERRY	SNAKE
BIRDS	SQUIRREL
BLOSSOM	TINSEL
CARVED INITIALS	TIRE ON A ROPE
INSECTS	TREE HOUSE
KITE	TWIG
KNOTHOLE	VINES

```
          H E T O
          O     K
          T S E N
            L T
          G A C C
      S Q U I R R E L
    A H T E T W K B S M
    P M I U I A T E A N
  E P O R A N O E R I T I
  S L S F S I S L R T I S
  R E S E A D S O Y E N A
  N S O T R E E H O U S E
    D L I N V L T G E E
    O B I M R E O I T L
      V K R A B N R K
        E C E K
```

5. 2, 4, 6, 8

Every item in the word list contains the consecutive letters TWO, FOUR, SIX, or EIGHT. But in the grid, these letters appear as the numbers 2, 4, 6, or 8. So, for example, CLINT EASTWOOD in the word list appears as CLINTEAS2OD in the grid. We hope you appreciate this puzzle. ("2, 4, 6, 8, who do we appreciate?") The hidden message is a sentence with more number-filled words.

AIRFREIGHT
ARTWORK
CLINT EASTWOOD
"DAYS OF OUR LIVES"
DEEP-SIX
DRIFTWOOD
EIGHTH NOTE
FOUR OF A KIND
FOUR-POSTER
FOURSOME

HEIGHTEN
NETWORKS
OVERWEIGHT
PETIT FOURS
SIXTH SENSE
SLEIGHT OF HAND
"[SING A] SONG OF SIXPENCE"
TWO-BY-FOURS
UNTRUSTWORTHY
WEIGHT LIFT

A P O S T E R

```
    4  P  O  S  T  E  R
 A  S  T  2  B  Y  4  S  U  N
 U  N  T  R  U  S  2  R  T  H  Y  O
 2  M  D  A  Y  S  O  4  L  I  V  E  S
 A  N  O  N           A  E  T  D  F
                      R  R  R  E  T
                W  8  I  A  F  P
          6  E  8  R  F  R  I  A
 R  F  I  T  8  R  2  2  L  E
 4  N  E  8  H  D  O  W  8
 S  H  E  N  S  D  K  W
 O  K  O  R  E
 M  T  R  D  N  A  H  F  O  8  L  S  6
 E  D  O  2  S  A  E  T  N  I  L  C  G
 U  E  C  N  E  P  6  F  O  G  N  O  S
 6  P  E  E  D  N  I  K  A  F  O  4  N
```

6. POOL PARTY

Shaped like a girl's one-piece bathing suit, the grid contains words associated with being at an outdoor swimming pool. The hidden message answers the riddle "Why did the boy who couldn't swim bring a kitchen sink to the pool party?"

BELLY FLOP

CHLORINE

COLD

DEEP END

DIVE

DUNK

FILTER

GOGGLES

LANES

LAPS

LOTION

MARCO POLO

MOUTHFUL

NOODLE

SPLASH

SWIMMING

TOWEL

TRUNKS

WADE

WATER WINGS

```
H                       E
S                       E
W                       N
  I K               N I
  M E W         S C R
  M A R C O P O L O
  I O I W L L T P L
  N W U A D A S O H
  G E S T O W E L C
    H P E H D I F
    T A R A F T Y
    D L W H R U L
    I U I U E S L
  R V D N E P E E D
  R E K G K S L B I
  L S T S N D G K O
    A R L O S G W
    I N O I T O L
    N E M F G
        S
```

7. CAN YOU STAND IT?

Shaped like a flamingo standing on one leg, the grid contains things you stand on. The hidden message is a rhyming answer to the question "What do you call an upside-down balancing act performed where a group of musicians play?"

BALCONY

BASE

BATH MAT

[THE] BRINK

CHAIR

CURB

DECK

DUTY

GROUND

[YOUR] HANDS

[YOUR] HEAD

LADDER

LINE

MOUNTAINTOP

PLATFORM

SCALE

SKIS

STILTS

SUBWAY

TIPTOE

```
        I  T  D  S
     A  E  S  A  B
  B  A     E  N
        L  H
     A  A
     C  N        D  S  T  G  C
  S  D     L  A  D  D  E  R  A  H  N
  S  U  B  W  A  Y  D  Y  N  O  C  L  A  B  H
  A  T  E  R  N  S  K  I  S  U  I  K  N  I  R  B
     Y  M  O  U  N  T  A  I  N  T  O  P  D  R
        S  T  C  T  I  E  D  E  C  K
           P           L
           I           T
           T           S
     M  R  O  F  T  A  L  P
     A           M
                 H
                 T
                 A
        N  D  B
```

8. MY I

Shaped like a head and stalk of broccoli, the grid contains words that end in the letter I. The hidden message contains three foods that also end with an I.

BIKINI

CACTI

CINCINNATI

FIJI

HIBACHI

HIPPOPOTAMI

HOI POLLOI

IRAQI

JACUZZI

MAHIMAHI

MIAMI

MINI

MISSISSIPPI

PARCHEESI

PEPPERONI

RAVIOLI

SAFARI

SALAMI

SCI-FI

SHANGHAI

SPAGHETTI

SUSHI

TAHITI

TAXI

YETI

```
            S  I  I  Z
         S  H  P  U  Z  I
      C  A  A  I  A  S  Z  C
      M  H  N  F  E  G  I  U
   F  I  J  I  G  E  A  I  H  F  C  C
T  H  N  K  R  H  N  I  R  C  E  I  A  A
L  A  A  I  H  C  A  B  I  H  I  M  T  C  J  A
M  X  B  M  R  H  I  V  I  T  I  H  A  T  S  M
R  I  I  A  C  I  N  C  I  N  N  A  T  I  I  A
N     P        P  D  M  O  O  S        S     O
      E     P  U  I  L  V  L        S
         P  O  S  A  L  A  M  I
         P  Y  M  O  L  S
         O  E  I  P  S  S
         T  T  R  I  A  U
         A  I  P  O  K  S
         M  P  I  H  N  H
         I  Q  A  R  I  I
```

9. BLOWHARDS

Shaped like a whirling tornado, the grid contains words associated with the wind. The hidden message answers the question "What did the pitcher on the girls' softball team do when it got really breezy?"

BLOW	STORM
BREEZE	SWIRL
CYCLONE	TORNADO
GALE	TURBULENCE
GUST	TWISTER
HOWL	TYPHOON
HURRICANE	UPDRAFT
JET STREAM	WESTERLY
NOR'EASTER	WHIP
SQUALL	WHIRLWIND

```
        E J S T H
      E W Z E E Y N P G
    W H T E T I P I L N U
  T O O U E S H H W E R W S
  I S S L R T W O D A N R O T
    N T Q B R H O D C E L U U
      P O U E I N Y T W R I
        T R A R C S H B I T
          M L I A U H W
          O W L L N E S
        N T I E U Y E
      E O W N P L
      L R C D R
      A E R E
    I G A T
    N F S
    T E T
    W D E
    U P R
```

10. TEAM PLAYERS

Shaped like a football helmet, the grid contains the team name for a player on each of the 32 teams in the National Football League. Twenty-six of those team players appear in the word list and should be circled in the grid as usual. The remaining six can be found in alphabetical order in the hidden message.

BEAR	DOLPHIN	RAVEN
BILL	EAGLE	REDSKIN
BRONCO	FORTY-NINER	SAINT
BROWN	GIANT	SEAHAWK
BUCCANEER	LION	STEELER
CARDINAL	PACKER	TEXAN
CHARGER	PANTHER	TITAN
CHIEF	PATRIOT	VIKING
COWBOY	RAIDER	

```
      B C O W B O Y
    R L L O C N O R B E
  F N A L N I H P L O D K
    R E N I N Y T R O F W B G
A L O I B D E E L G A E N C
B I O D H L E V C H A R G E R
L U T R N C F R A R A
L G C A       C E O R
N N T C       S K N
J I G I A N T C A
T K K G U N E A
  I A S I A E P A T R I O T R
  V J A D X L E E           T
  S R A E E   R E H T N A P
      M T R
```

11. PLAY GROUND

Shaped like home plate in baseball, the grid contains things you might find on the ground—in the city, the country, or elsewhere. The hidden message is one more playful thing that would fit nicely on this list.

AUTUMN LEAVES

BEACH BLANKET

BUGS

DIRT

GRASS

GRAVEL

HAY BALES

HOME PLATE

LITTER

LOST COINS

MANHOLE COVER

PUDDLES

RAILROAD TRACKS

ROCKS

SIDEWALKS

SNAKE

SNOW

SQUIRREL

TACKLED PLAYER

WAD OF GUM

WEEDS

WORMS

S K C A R T D A O R L I A R H
N T E K N A L B H C A E B A A
O R E V O C E L O H N A M G Y
W P S N A K E B E R S M R O B
S E V A E L N M U T U A E N A
D I R T L E V A R G S W T H L
O S D M A D W K F S S I T N E
S D E E W P L O S T C O I N S
  Q G A W L D S R N O R L E
    U E T A L P E M O H L
      I W Y L W A C S D
        R E N K K G D
        R E S S U
        E L P
         L

12. THE SOUND OF MUSIC

Shaped like an electric guitar, the grid contains places, activities, and things in, at, or on which you hear music being played. The hidden message answers the riddle "What did the girl do with her sheet music from band practice?"

CAROUSEL

CELL PHONE

CHURCH

CONCERT

DANCE

ELEVATOR

FINAL JEOPARDY

MALL

MOVIE

MUSICAL

PARADE

PARTY

STORE

VIDEO GAME

```
        F C
      S I E H
        N L
    M A L L
        L P
        J H
        E O
E       O N
P       P E       U
T I     A M       T
E I C R A     M N
H C O D G P U E
R L N Y O A S
  E C A E R I
  S E N D A C O
T U R I I D A E
R O T A V E L E
B R O S T O R E
P A R T Y O M K
  C H U R C H
```

13. WINGING IT

Shaped like an angel in profile, the grid contains things with wings. The hidden message completes this question: "Would you rather be bitten by horseflies or by Pegasus…"

ANGELS	LARK
BATS	MOTH
BIPLANE	MUSEUM
CONDORS	ROBIN
DRAGON	SPARROW
FLIES	TINKERBELL
GLIDER	TURKEY
HOTEL	VULTURE
ICARUS	[THE] WHITE HOUSE
LADYBUG	WREN

```
    S  T  A  B
          N
          G
    A     L  E
 K  R  A  L
 H  D  S
    Y        D  M  V
 O  E  B  E  R  R  U  S  F
 S  S  U  A  K  L  S  N  L  E
 T  U  G  W  T  R  E  D  I  L  G
 I  O  R  U  R  N  U  T  E  B  H
 N  H  R  A  A  E  M  T  S  T  O  H
 K  E  S  L  C  O  N  D  O  R  S  R  A
 E  T  P  E     I     M     T     F
 R  I  A  T
 B  H  R  O
 E  W  R  H
 L  L  O  I
 L  E  W  S
```

14. IT'S ONLY MONEY

Shaped like a dollar sign, the grid contains words and images that are printed on various denominations of United States currency. The hidden message completes the joke that begins "Did you hear about the girl who was saving for a rainy day?"

AMERICA

CAPITOL

CENTS

DEBTS

E PLURIBUS UNUM

EYES

FLAG

[THE] GREAT SEAL

KENNEDY

LIBERTY

NOTE

PYRAMID

STARS

TORCH

TREASURY

UNITED STATES

WASHINGTON

[THE] WHITE HOUSE

```
            U  S
            N  O
      W  A  S  H  I  N  G  T  O  N  O
   N  L  A  E  S  T  A  E  R  G  S  H
   T  I  E  T  L  E  M  L  B  E  A  B
   O  B  N        D  U
   R  E  L        S  N
   C  R  E        T  U
   H  T  T  R  E  A  S  U  R  Y  E
   T  Y  O  O  A  T  U  S  T  A  R  S
      F  N  F  D  E  B  T  S  C  O  E
               S  I        I  R  Y
               D  R        R  D  E
               A  U        E  N  U
   C  A  P  I  T  O  L  M  N  M  B  R
   D  I  M  A  R  Y  P  N  G  A  L  F
   E  E  S  U  O  H  E  T  I  H  W
               K  L
               L  A
```

15. IN A FIX

Shaped like a pump at a gas station, the grid contains things a car might have problems with—and why it might be brought into a gas station. The hidden message is a sign that a gas station owner with a sense of humor might put up next to his pumps.

ANTIFREEZE	HORN
BACKFIRES	LEAK
BATTERY	MUFFLER
BRAKES	PAINT JOB
DENTS	RADIO
DISCS	RATTLING
ENGINE	SHIMMY
EXHAUST	SMOKE
FILTER	STEERING
FUEL	TIRES
GEARS	TRANSMISSION
HEAT	WIPERS

```
W  E  X  H  A  U  S  T
G  N  I  L  T  T  A  R
E                 A  A
G                 N     E
E                 S  I     G
N  R  E  L  F  F  U  M  T     V
I  E  G  R  S  E  S  I     N  A
G  N  I  R  E  E  T  S        E
N  E  T  N  R  O  H  S           D
E  Z  S  I  I  E  M  I           I
P  E  T  D  F  O  L  O           S
A  E  A  F  K  S  S  N           C
I  R  E  E  C  A  R  R           S
N  F  B  R  A  K  E  S        H
T  I  U  H  B  V  P  L     I
J  T  R  E  T  L  I  F  M
O  N  I  A  L  C  W  M
B  A  T  T  E  R  Y  E
```

16. AW, CHUTE!

Shaped like a parachute, the grid contains words associated with skydiving. The hidden message is a new, funny ending for the old saying that begins "If at first you don't succeed..."

ALTITUDE

CANOPY

CHUTE

FLOAT

FREEFALL

HARNESS

JUMP

LANDING

LOOP

PLANE

PULL

RIPCORD

SKYDIVING

SOLO

SPIN

STATIC LINE

TANDEM

WIND

```
            M   E   D   G   O
        N   E   T   T   N   H   L   T   N
    E   D   U   T   I   T   L   A   I   A   T
A   N   H   K   D   J   U   M   P   R   E   O   U
P   A   C   A   N   O   P   Y   S   P   E   N   A   L   P
T   A   R   A   P   O   O   L   L   A   F   E   E   R   F
S   O   L   O           A   R   C           H   U   S   T
I                       I                               S
    S                   P                       T
        K               C                   A
            Y           O               T
                D       R           I
                    I   D       C
                    V   N   L
                        I
                    N   W   N
                E   N       G   G
```

In "Alice in Wonderland," the Queen of Hearts commanded, "Off with her head!" So we took the queen to heart and cut off the word HEAD in every word or phrase in the head-shaped grid. For example, the word HEADQUARTERS in the list will appear only as QUARTERS in the grid. Don't let it go to your HEAD, but the hidden message will tell you four more words that can end with HEAD.

BLOCKHEAD

COME TO A HEAD

DOUBLEHEADER

HARDHEADED

HEADACHES

HEADDRESS

HEADFIRST

HEAD FOR COVER

HEADGEAR

HEADHUNTER

HEADLESS

HORSEMAN

HEADLIGHTS

HEAD LINESMAN

HEADMASTER

HEAD OF LETTUCE

HEAD OVER HEELS

HEADQUARTERS

HEADROOM

HEADS OR TAILS

HEADSPACE

HEADSTART

HEADSTRONG

HIT THE NAIL ON THE HEAD

HOTHEADED

MEATHEAD

PIGHEADED

SHOWERHEAD

SOREHEAD

```
            S  K  S  N  U
         C  F  O  R  C  O  V  E  R
      O  K  L  R  E  H  L  R  H  G  D
      A  F  E  E  F  I  R  S  T  E  E
      M  T  L  M  N  E  E  O  N  A  G
R     S  L  E  E  H  R  E  V  O  R  I     S
L  A  Q  E  S     T  E  L     L  M  P  L  P
M  Y  U  M  S  D  A  T  B  L  I  G  H  T  S
N  D  A  C  H  E  S     U  K  A  D  S  T  G
   N  R  A  O  T  E  M  O  C  N  H  H  N
   T  E  R  O  H  U  D  O  E  A  O
   E  C  S  H           L  H  R  W
   R  A  E  S           B  T  D  E
   S  P  M  T           S  T  E  R
   S  A  A              N  I  D
   D  N  R  E  T  N  U  H  E
      T  A  E  M  R
```

18. JUMP FOR JOY

Shaped like a hopscotch board, the grid contains things you jump or jump over. The hidden message answers the riddle "Why do you need to calm down when you play checkers?"

A LOG
CANDLESTICK
CHECKER
CRACK
DITCH
FENCE
HEDGE
HIGH BAR
HOPSCOTCH SQUARE
HURDLE

LEAPFROG PLAYER
PUDDLE
RAILING
ROPE
SHIP
STREAM
TENNIS NET
THE GUN
TURNSTILE
WALL

```
        P L R
      A Y E R W
      I K A E A
      C B C Y L
N S E H G A A L O G A
D H G O E N L R N G A
C I M P P D P U C M E
H P T S O L G T A C A
      C R E O E
      O H S R N
      T E T F N
      C S I P I
N M N H A C A S K E Y
O E U S H K E N F E R
F E P Q U L L E K A I
N D T U R N S T I L E
      A D O F L
      R L D I J
      E E N L U
      M G P Y E
```

19. A TALL TALE

Shaped like a giraffe, the grid contains things that are or may be tall. The hidden message answers the riddle "Which Major League Baseball team is the tallest?"

ALPS	ORDER
EIFFEL TOWER	SHIP
ELEPHANT	SKYSCRAPER
FLAGPOLE	SPHINX
GODZILLA	TALE
GOLIATH	TREE
LADDER	T. REX
MAST	WALL
N.B.A. PLAYER	

```
        I       H
        T       T
    T S P L A
  S A T H E I
  M       F       L
          L       O
          A       G
          G       O
          P       D
          O       Z
        G L I L I A S T
        R E L E P H A N T
        E A L N I L T R E X
        W T A P E R E E S N
        O   D       E   P       I
        T   D       Y   A       H
        L   E       A   R       P
        E   R       L   C       S
        F   E       P   S
        F   D       A   Y
        I   R       B   K
        E   O       N   S
```

45

20. THAT'S NEWS TO ME!

Shaped like a TV with a cable box on top, the grid contains people and things you might hear about on the evening news. The hidden message is a comment about the news that begins "The things that happened today are pretty much the same as yesterday…"

ACCIDENT	GLOBAL WARMING	SENATOR
CELEBRITIES	HERO	SPACE MISSION
CRIME	MOVIES	SPORTS
DISCOVERY	PRESIDENT	STORM
EARTHQUAKE	PROTESTS	STYLES
ECONOMY	REFORMS	TIME
ELECTION	RESCUE	TRAFFIC
FIRE	SCANDAL	TRIAL
FLOOD		

```
            S  M  R  O  F  E  R
            E  O  X  C  M  E  P
R  T  H  T  H  V  D  I  L  A  D  N  A  C  S
O  A  E  S  E  I  T  I  R  B  E  L  E  C  T
T  T  R  T  H  E  U  C  S  E  R  K  E  Y  S
A  N  O  I  S  S  I  M  E  C  A  P  S  H  E
N  A  E  P  E  F  P  L  R  U  O  T  E  N  T
E  E  M  D  F  C  E  D  Q  O  Y  V  T  S  O
S  T  I  A  I  C  O  H  O  L  T  D  E  T  R
I  F  R  F  T  C  T  N  E  D  I  S  E  R  P
E  T  C  I  R  R  C  S  O  R  E  N  T  O  Y
G  L  O  B  A  L  W  A  R  M  I  N  G  P  P
E  N  O  E  F  L  O  O  D  P  Y  F  L  S  E
```

21. HOT STUFF

Shaped like a sombrero hat, the grid contains foods found in a Mexican restaurant. The hidden message is a punny weather report that could appear on a Mexican Food Channel.

BEANS	HUEVOS
BURRITO	JALAPENO
CHALUPA	LECHE
CHILI	NACHOS
ENCHILADA	RICE
FAJITA	SALSA
FLAN	SOPE
FLAUTA	TACO
GORDITA	TORTILLA
GUACAMOLE	TOSTADA

```
            I  T
         L  L  L  E
         B  E  E  N
      T  T  C  C  C
      S  O  P  E  H  H
      A  R  S  I  I  E
      L  T  L  T  L  I
L  H  U  E  V  O  S  I  I  I  A  G  O  R  D  I  T  A
T  O  O  N  E  P  A  L  A  J  D  D  I  B  E  A  N  S
D  N  A  L  F  A  E  L  O  M  A  C  A  U  G  Y  A  N
   C  H  A  L  U  P  A  D  H  E  F  O  R  T  T  A
      A                          R
      U                          I
      T                          T
      A  M                    A  O
         A  L              C  E
            N  A  C  H  O  S
```

49

22. CLEAN UP YOUR ACT

Shaped like a washing machine with a box of detergent on top, the grid contains things you clean with. The hidden message answers the riddle "Why did the bank robbers use soap and water during the holdup?"

BROOM
CLOTH
COTTON BALLS
DETERGENT
DISHWASHER
DUST RAGS
FLOSS
HOSE
MOPS
PAPER TOWEL

POLISH
Q-TIPS
SCOURING PAD
SHAMPOO
SOAP
SPONGE
SQUEEGEE
TOOTHPASTE
VACUUM CLEANER
WATER

```
        T D H
        H U E
        S S H
        C T I
V Y O R W L H M A P M
A L U A N T O O E A O
C D R G Q T I P S P O
U D I S H W A S H E R
U E N T O M A K A R B
M T G E           A M T C
C E P             P O E
L R A             O W E
E G D R           L O E G
A E E E A S F N G L E
N N E T O T A L W A E
E T S A P H T O O T U
R Y P W E G N O P S Q
C O T T O N B A L L S
```

23. FOWL PLAY

Shaped like a Christmas tree, the grid contains words and phrases from the popular holiday song "The Twelve Days of Christmas." The hidden message completes this thought: "Except for the fifth day of Christmas, the first seven days weren't so hot. In fact, when you think about it, you could say…"

CALLING BIRDS	MAIDS
DANCING	PARTRIDGE
DAYS	PEAR
DRUMMERS	PIPERS
FRENCH HENS	SENT
GEESE	SWANS
GOLDEN RINGS	TO ME
LADIES	TREE
LORDS	TRUE
LOVE	TURTLE DOVES

```
                    R
                  T   H   A
                G   E   E   S   E
              S   E   I   D   A   L   P
            E   P   Y   I   W   S   Y   A   D
                A   E   D   R   E
              M   S   R   E   P   I   P
            E   M   O   T   T   R   E   E   F
          G   O   L   D   E   N   R   I   N   G   S
        C   A   L   L   I   N   G   B   I   R   D   S   O
              G   N   I   C   N   A   D
            L   R   S   W   A   N   S   T   G
          O   D   R   U   M   M   E   R   S   H   E
        V   E   B   F   R   E   N   C   H   H   E   N   S
    E   U   R   T   U   R   T   L   E   D   O   V   E   S   I
                    R
                    D
                    S
```

24. HOW SWEET IT IS

Shaped like a honey-bear-shaped bottle of honey, the grid contains things that are sweet. The hidden message completes the joke "The diet doctor told me I can't have ice cream for dessert anymore…"

ANIMAL CRACKERS	FUDGE	PEACH
BAKLAVA	ICING	PEANUT BRITTLE
BROWNIE	JAMS	PIES
CAKES	JUJUBES	SUCKER
COTTON CANDY	MAPLE SYRUP	SUGAR
CUSTARD	NOUGAT	TAFFY
DONUT	OREOS	TART
ECLAIR	PARFAIT	TOFFEE
FLAN		

```
                S
                R
        O   R   E   O   S
        S   S   K   I   O
        R   E   K   C   U   S   P
    N   I   R   I   A   L   C   E   O
    P   Y   N   T   R   S   M   A   J
        G   F   O   C   E   A   C
        W   I   F   L   L   P   H
        L   F   A   T   L
        A   C   E   M   T   E   H
    N   A   O   E   I   I   S   V   T
    J   E   T   I   N   R   Y   A   U
    U   N   T   W   A   B   R   C   N
    J   T   O   A   S   T   U   U   O
    U   R   N   U   S   U   P   S   D
    B   C   C   A   G   N   G   T   N
    E   B   A   K   L   A   V   A   A
    S   G   N   K   P   E   T   R   R
        P   D   E   E   P   T   D
        I   Y   U   Z   S   E   R
        P   A   R   F   A   I   T
```

25. TAKE A BREAK

Shaped like a heart, the grid contains things you break. The hidden message answers the riddle "Why did the bully punch the pleading boy hard in the nose?"

A TIE

[A] BAD HABIT

[A] BLISTER

CAMP

[THE] CASE

[THE] CODE

[YOUR]
  CONCENTRATION

EGGS

[A] FAST

[SOMEONE'S]
  HEART

[A] NAIL

[THE] NEWS

PEANUT BRITTLE

[A] PROMISE

RANK

[THE] RULES

SHOELACES

[THE] SKIN

[THE] SOIL

[A] SPELL

[SOMEONE'S]
  SPIRIT

[A] STREAK

[A] SWEAT

THE LAW

[A] TOOTH

[A] TRUCE

WATER BALLOONS

[A] WINDOW

[A] WISHBONE

[THE] WORLD
  RECORD

B W E   C N A

P U I S E   W A H E E

R R E S A C R   E I I S K W A

E O I H G D U   L W C N I K S

T M S B C G L   T O A H D O M

S I C O N C E N T R A T I O N

I S D N I E S W I L S O T O W

L E H E N L A G R D P O R I S

B S N O O L L A B R E T A W V

A K A E R T S T E L C E E

D H I L M S U C L A H

T H T E A E N O T M A

I A F B C A R R P

R B E U E D A

I I R P S

P T K

S

26. TOOLING ALONG

Shaped like a handsaw propped up on its handle, the grid contains different kinds of tools. The hidden message completes the old joke "'It's a miracle!' said the blind man, as he…"

AUGER	PINCERS
AWLS	PLIERS
BOLT	RIVETER
CHISEL	SANDER
DRILL	SCREW
FILE	SOLDERING IRON
HACKSAW	TROWEL
HAMMER	VISE
LATHE	WIRE CUTTER
NAIL	WRENCH

```
            F  I  L  E
            R  L  A
         H  I  E  T  E
            R  V  S  H
      D  L  E  I  E  D
         R  R  T  H  S
         E  E  E  C  O  E
   P  M  T  R  U  L
   L  M  T  S  H  D  P
   I  A  U  A  A  E
   H  E  H  C  N  E  R  W
   A  R  K  E  D  M  I
   M  S  C  R  E  W  N  E
R  A  A  N  I  R  D  G
W  U     A  W  L  S  I  S
   G                 R  A
   E                 O
T  R  O  W  E  L  W  N
L  S  R  E  C  N  I  P
O                    A
B                    N
```

27. HURRY UP AND GET DOWN TO BUSINESS

Every item in the word list contains the letters UP or DOWN in consecutive order. When these letters appear in the up-and-down-arrow grid, every UP has been replaced by ⬆ and every DOWN by ⬇. For example, the UPSIDE-DOWN will appear as ⬆ SIDE ⬇. So pick ⬆ your pencil and get ⬇ to it. The hidden message is what an angry grown ⬆ might say when dressing ⬇ a misbehaving child.

ACT UP	ERUPT	UPFRONT
BUCKLE UP	GANG UP ON	UPROAR
DOWN-AND-OUT	RUBDOWN	UPSET
DOWNLOAD	SUNDOWN	UPSIDE-DOWN
DOWNPOUR	SUPERMAN	UPTIGHT
DOWN-TO-EARTH	TOUCHDOWN	UP TO NO GOOD
DOWNTOWN	UP AND AT 'EM	UPWIND
DOWNWARD	UPDATE	"WHAT'S UP, DOC?"

```
                    B
              ↓   ↑  U
           S  P  I  T  C
           ↑  R  O  A  R  I  K
           ↓  H  C  U  O  T  T  G  L
     T  T  N  O  R  F  ↑  U  ↓  H  E
  ↓  L  O  A  D  O  O  G  O  N  O  T  ↑
           ↑  W  I  N  D
           S  U  N  ↓  N
           T  ↑  M  H  A
           A  A  E  T  ↓
           H  N  T  R  E
  D  D  R  A  W  ↓  A  A  M  S  S  H  G
     U  T  ↑  S  I  D  E  ↓  A  ↑  A
        ↓  T  O  W  N  O  C  ↑  N
           B  ↑  D  A  T  E  G
           U  R  ↑  ↓  ↑
           R  E  O
           N
```

28. ROLL CALL

Shaped like a shopping cart, the grid contains things that roll or are rolled. The hidden message answers the riddle "Why did the good-looking, hard-working girls want to star in a Rollerblade commercial?"

BALL	NEWSPAPER
BUGGY	PLAY-DOH
COINS	PULL TOY
DICE	SKATEBOARD
DOLLY	STEAMROLLER
DOUGH	TANK
[YOUR] EYES	THUNDER
GOLF CART	TIRE
GURNEY	TUMBLEWEED
LAWN MOWER	WAGON
LUGGAGE	

```
T  L  P
   B  U  G  G  Y  R  E  P  A  P  S  W  E  N
   Y  L  G  H  P  H  E  L  Y  T  W  A  A  N
      L  T  G  L  E  D  L  E  T  O  G  B
      T  L  U  A  T  R  A  C  F  L  O  G
      O  E  O  Y  G  M  B  C  O  I  N  S
      Y  R  D  D  R  E  D  N  U  H  T  S
      D  R  A  O  B  E  T  A  K  S  E
         O  L  H  G  U  R  N  E  Y  L
         L  A  W  N  M  O  W  E  R
      E
   R  L  V  T  U  M  B  L  E  W  E  E  D
         A  M                 O  C
      D  N  W  E            E  R  I  T
         K  L               S  D
```

29. STRIP SEARCH

Shaped like a speech balloon, the grid contains the names of characters from syndicated newspaper comic strips. The hidden message answers this quiz: "What title characters of two popular comic strips—a cat and a duck—have the same names as two former presidents of the United States?"

ARLO
BLONDIE
CATHY
CROCK
CURTIS
DOGBERT
ELLY PATTERSON
HAGAR
HEATHCLIFF
HERMAN
LOIS

LUANN
MOOSE
NANCY
ODIE
ROSE
SALLY FORTH
SHOE
SNOOPY
TINA
[THE] WIZARD OF ID
ZIGGY

```
      E I D N O L B
    I G Z N A N R O F
  D D I F O D R A Z I W
O O G I E S I T R U C S E
L G A H T R O F Y L L A S
Y B H N D E M O O S E H O
A E N A I T K D N M E A R
L R L M G T C O A A O Y R
  T D R F A O I T L H L
    M E O P R H R T S
      H Y Y C N A N
        L O C
        I L E
      F R E
    F A
```

30. GOING PLACES

Shaped like a home, the grid contains places you might go to during the course of a typical day. The hidden message mentions another place you might go, but not as often and only when you play.

BACKYARD

BASEMENT

BUS STOP

CAFETERIA

CLASS

CLOSET

FRIEND'S HOUSE

GARAGE

GROCERY

HOME

KITCHEN

LAVATORY

LIBRARY

MALL

MOVIES

ON-LINE

OUTSIDE

PARK

PLAYGROUND

SCHOOL

STORE

YOUR ROOM

```
            I
          L N N
        I A M O E
      B N V O R C H
    R F P A O O L L C
  A I R E T E F A C Y T
R T H I S O G E S O P P I
Y B Y E N R A L S L A Y   K
  A R N P Y R L A R A C
  S E D D R A Y K C A B
  E C S E T G O G T O U
  M O H I R S P E A S S
  E R O O U T S I D E S
  N G U R O O K E P I T
  T N S L L L A M M V O
  D A E C E N I L N O P
  C E Y O U R R O O M H
```

31. SHAKE ON IT

Shaped like a snow globe, the grid contains things you shake. The hidden message is a punny warning relating to the shape.

A COLD	JELL-O
A FIST AT	JUICE CARTON
A LEG	MARACAS
APPLE TREE	POMPOMS
BABY BOTTLE	RATTLE
BELL	SALT SHAKER
BOGGLE	SNOW GLOBE
DICE	TAMBOURINE
ETCH-A-SKETCH	WRAPPED GIFT
HANDS	YOUR HEAD

```
      H O L D L
    E E R T E L P P A
  T F I G D E P P A R W
I N G S A B S N D O L W B
G L T A M B O U R I N E O
O B E L C A H B A N C M G
A H C T E K S A H C T E G
A F I S T A T B N K O E L
D A E H R U O Y Y D O L E
M A R A C A S B U F S E D
  E L K R S M O P M O P
    E E R A T T L E A
    R L L Y T S L
  H S N O W G L O B E A
K N O T R A C E C I U J Y
```

32. THAT'S STRETCHING IT

Shaped like a Slinky toy walking down stairs, the grid contains things you stretch or that stretch. The hidden message answers the riddle "What would a contortionist say is his favorite part of a baseball game?"

ACCORDION

[YOUR] BACK

BALLOON

BOWSTRING

BUBBLE GUM

BUNGEE CORD

CANVAS

COASTLINE

ELASTIC

HOSE

[YOUR] LEGS

LYCRA

[YOUR] MIND

ROPE

RUBBER BAND

SILLY PUTTY

SLINKY

SNAKE

TAFFY

[THE] TRUTH

WINGS

YOGI

```
        S Y K I T B S S
      N F K C T U H G E B
    A F D N A B R E B B U R
  K A S W I B A L L O O N G
E T S I L L Y P U T T Y G N E
L V N E E S       N T I E I A
A G H G A         E G E R C
S D U V I         N O C T C
T M N N N         I Y O S O
I A I I N         L G R W R
C S T R M         T E D O D
                  S R P B I
                  A E U T O
                  O C H T N
                  C E S O H
```

33. MISSION TO MARS

Shaped like the planet Mars, the grid contains words and phrases associated with exploring that planet. The hidden message is a riddle and its answer about a manned mission to Mars.

BOULDERS

CAMERAS

DEIMOS

DUST

EARTH'S NEIGHBOR

EXPLORATION

GLOBAL SURVEYOR

GULLY

GUSEV CRATER

HEMATITE

HILLS

ICE CAP

LIFE?

MARTIANS?

PHOBOS

PROBE

RED PLANET

ROCKS

ROVERS

SAND

SOIL

SPACE MISSION

TWO MOONS

WATER?

```
            W  P  R  O  B  E
      H  D  A          A  F  T
   K  I  U  N          R  D  I  O
R  G  U  S  E  V  C  R  A  T  E  R  L  S
B  E  F  T  E  D  C  O  A  H  N  D  P  H
Y  O  W  D  I  X  N  L  V  L  S  W  A  T  E  R
A  U  S  T  P  P  A  R  E  A  N  C  O  N  M  A
G  L  O  B  A  L  S  U  R  V  E  Y  O  R  A  U
T  D  M  P  S  O  A  E  S  M  I  E  A  T  T  H
W  E  H  A  E  R  M  N  I  N  G  T  S  W  I  H
E  R  Y  C  R  A  S  S  E  U  H  O  O  L  T  D
   S  G  E  C  T  S  K  L  T  B  M  L  E  E
   T  O  C  H  I  I  L  C  O  O  S  E  I  R
      E  I  O  O  Y  A  H  O  R  M  M  A
      N  L  N  R  P  N  S  R  O  B
         A  R  S  S  S  S
```

34. JUST SAY NO

Every item in the word list contains the letters NO in consecutive order. When these letters appear in the grid, each NO has been replaced by a "Halt!" sign ✋ meaning "No!" Be sure to TAKE ✋TE that the grid's shape resembles a road sign with a slash mark, which indicates not to do something, like No U-Turn. But do turn to the hidden message, which you'll ✋TICE is a simple geographical fact.

BINOCULARS	MONOPOLY	NOZZLE
CANNONS	NOAH'S ARK	OBNOXIOUS
CANOE	NOBEL PRIZE	PHENOMENAL
CASINOS	"NOBODY'S HOME!"	PINOCCHIO
EQUINOX	NOISY	SNOOPY
GNOME	NO-NONSENSE	SNORED
"I KNOW NOTHING!"	NOUNS	"THAT'S A NO-NO!"
KNOBS	NOVEMBER	VENOM

G M [hand] E V E
[hand] B O D Y S H O M E
I K [hand] W [hand] T H I N G [hand] E
[hand] A P I   K E G K
E O O H S   [hand] R
[hand] L I S B E [hand]   B A T
Y Z H   R [hand] [hand] [hand]   E S C
[hand] Z C   A X M N   L H Y
X [hand] C   L I E S   P A S
R [hand] [hand]   U O N E   R [hand] I
Y T I   C U A N   I H [hand]
P P U   [hand] S L S Z D
O O F Q   I A [hand] E R
W [hand] V E M B E R C B R A
Y S T H A T S A [hand] [hand]
C A N [hand] N S

75

35. TAKING IT ALL IN

Shaped like a money bag, the grid contains things you take. The hidden message answers the riddle "Most people like to take, but what's something lots of people don't like to take?"

A BOW

A NAP

[A] BATH

[A] BREAK

[A] CHANCE

CHARGE

CONTROL

[A] DRINK

FIVE

[A] FOUL SHOT

[A] LOOK

[A] MESSAGE

[AN] OATH

[A] PHONE NUMBER

[A] PICTURE

[YOUR] PULSE

[A] QUIZ

[A] RIDE

SHELTER

[YOUR] SHOES OFF

[A] TEST

[YOUR] TIME

[A] VACATION

VITAMINS

[A] WALK

```
          S                 R

              N  E  Z

              S  I  E

              U  S  M

        P  Q  L  H  T  A  O

     F  O  U  L  S  H  O  T  R

     I  P  I  C  T  U  R  E  I

  F  V  H  O  P        N  L  H  D  V

  F  E  O  A           O  T  E  A

  O  S  N  K        E  G  R  A  H  C

  S  A  E  L           T  B  K  A

  E  C  N  A  H  C     N  O  N  T

  O  I  U  W           O  W  I  I

  H  B  M  I  T        L  C  M  R  O

  S  L  B  R  E  A  K  E  I  D  N

     M  E  S  S  A  G  E  T  Y

        R  E  T  L  E  H  S
```

36. HOLD ON!

Shaped like a cell phone, the grid contains things you hold. The hidden message answers the riddle "What did the Olympic weight lifter say weighs absolutely nothing but is the hardest thing to hold?"

BABY

[YOUR] BREATH

CELL PHONE

COMB

CONVERSATION

DOLL

[YOUR] FIRE

FORK

GOLF CLUB

GRUDGE

HANDS

[YOUR] HORSES

[YOUR] NOSE

OPINION

PENCIL

POLITICAL OFFICE

STILL

[YOUR] TEMPER

[YOUR] TONGUE

TOOTHBRUSH

```
                        P
                        O
                        L
    A   H   T   A   E   R   B   I   N
    N   S   T   I   L   L   E   T   O
    E   U   G   N   O   T   W   I   I
    R   R                   C   T
    I   B                   A   A
    F   H                   L   S
    G   T   W   B   O   G   K   O   R
    L   O   M   H   R   R   P   F   E
    I   O   L   U   O   I   R   F   V
    C   T   D   F   N   R   R   I   N
    N   G   N   I   C   E   S   C   O
    E   N   O   H   P   L   L   E   C
    P   N   S   M   L   L   U   D   S
    R   E   E   C   O   B   A   B   Y
    O   T   S   D   N   A   H   R   D
```

37. WATERLOGGED

Shaped like a drop of water, the grid contains words and phrases that all contain at least two H's and one O or H_2O, the chemical symbol for water. The hidden message is a sentence that contains three more "water"-filled words.

DISHCLOTH

FISHHOOK

FRENCH HORN

GHOULISH

HAND-TO-MOUTH

HEAVE-HO

HICCOUGH

HI-HO

HIP-HOP

HOGWASH

HO-HUM

HULA HOOP

OOMPAH-PAH

PHARAOH

ROUGHHOUSE

RUSH HOUR

SHILOH

SHOPAHOLIC

THOUGH

TOOTHBRUSH

WHITE-HOT

WHOOSH

WITHHOLD

```
                        D
                        I
                    P   S   T
                    O   H   I
                T   O   C   A   H
            O   U   M   L   U   R   G
            G   G   P   O   H   H   A
        H   H   H   A   T   T   T   I   O
    E   S   U   O   H   H   G   U   O   R   H
    S   U   L   U   P   S   A   O   W   K   O
H   W   R   A   L   A   A   O   M   O   P   L   H
E   I   B   H   I   H   G   U   O   C   C   I   H
A   T   H   O   S   O   T   H   T   H   O   H   G
V   H   T   O   H   R   H   A   D   H   W   S   R
E   H   O   P   P   S   H   O   N   I   F   U   A
H   O   O   C   I   L   O   H   A   P   O   H   S
O   L   T   F   R   E   N   C   H   H   O   R   N
    D   T   W   H   I   T   E   H   O   T   H
        H   O   G   W   A   S   H   P   O
            R   N   M   U   H   O   H
                B   R   U   S   H
```

38. PAY ATTENTION!

Shaped like a stop sign, the grid contains words and phrases that are often followed by an exclamation point. The hidden message is one more such exclamation, which appropriately comes at the very end.

AARGH!	LISTEN!	SHARKS!
BE QUIET!	NEVER!	SHOOT!
DARN!	NOT NOW!	STOP!
DUCK!	NO WAY!	THAT WAS CLOSE!
GET OUT!	NUTS!	WAIT!
GO TO YOUR ROOM!	OH, NO!	WATCH IT!
HELP!	OMIGOSH!	WHOA!
I'M MELTING!	PHEW!	YOU'RE A LIAR!
I OBJECT!	RATS!	

```
        W A I T I
      E A C C M N D
    H A M E M G E Y A
  P R O J E E N V O N R
O G O B L T S O E U K T N
H G O T O Y O U R R O O M
N I I U S L L H A E W O W
O N T K D I C H E A O H W
G M N O U S S C Y L K S S
  T I H C T A W N I P T
    I G K E W U T A A
    W O N T O N R
      O S A F F
        H
        T
        E
        I
        U
        Q
        E
        B
```

39. KNOCK IT OFF!

Shaped like stacked bottles in a carnival game, the grid contains games and other things associated with a carnival. The hidden message answers the riddle "What was the restless boy doing when he played ring toss while riding the merry-go-round?"

AIR RIFLE

BALLOON

BELL-RINGER

BOTTLES

BOWLS

BUCKET

CARNY

CAROUSEL

DARTS

DUCKS

DUNK

FISH

HORSE RACE

KEWPIE DOLL

MILK CANS

PITCH

POND

PRIZE

RIDES

RING TOSS

SQUIRT

THROWS

TIP THE CAT

TOY GUN

```
            T  S  O
               S
            S  O  S
         P  I  T  C  H
         C  D  G  I  H
         A  N  N  S  H
         R  I  I  O  T
         N  F  R  I  P
         Y  S  P  R  G
         E  T  A  S  I
   N  D  R  H        L  F  L  T
      A  E              W  L
   C  C  G  S           U  B  O  E
E  A  B  N  N  D     R  T  A  D  B  N
T  R  O  I  A  U     R  O  L  E  I  S
R  O  T  R  C  C     I  Y  L  I  P  W
I  U  T  L  K  K     D  G  O  P  R  O
U  S  L  L  L  S     E  U  O  W  I  R
Q  E  E  E  I  N     S  N  N  E  Z  H
S  L  S  B  M  G     B  U  C  K  E  T
```

40. WHAT SMELLS?

Shaped like a flower, the grid contains things that have distinctive odors. The hidden message offers three more things that definitely fit this description.

BACON

BAKERY

BARN

CIGAR

FUMES

INCENSE

LEMON

LICORICE

MINT

ORANGE

PERFUME

POPCORN

SEA AIR

SEWER

SHAMPOO

SKUNK

```
                    T
        F           N               I
    E       S       I       S               H
        G   F   U   M   E   S       P
            N   M   I   A   A   R   O
            K   E   A   A   N   T   P   F
        R   E   C   I   R   O   C   I   L   E   S
            R   A   H   O   L   E   A
            B   U   R   P   N   D   N
        R       N   O   M   E   L       S
    Y           A       A       N           E
            D           H       B
    E                   S                       N
    M   S               K           C   O
    A   U   E           U           I   C   D
        B   F   W       N       G   A   R
            Y   R   E   K   A   B   E
            A   E   R   T   H
                    P
```

87

41. MARKING ON THE CURVE

Shaped like an arched doorway, the grid contains things that are always or often curved. The hidden message completes this riddle and answer: "Why did the dishonest athlete curl up the referee's rule book? Because he wanted…"

BANANA

BOOMERANG

CRESCENT MOON

CURLICUE

DOME

FISHHOOK

HAWK'S BEAK

HORSESHOE

LENS

[THE] LETTER C

RAINBOW

RIBS

RING

ROAD

SKIS

ST. LOUIS ARCH

SWAN'S NECK

TUBE

TUNING FORK

TUSK

```
        L E T T E R C
      A N A N A B I T H
    R A I N B O W B O O B
  N E S T L O U I S A R C H
  O N C D M       T U S K A
K O S U E         T E F W H
R M W R           S I K E
O T A L           H S S E
F N N I           O H B M
G E S C           E H E O
N C N U           R O A D
I S E E           R O K R
N E C B           S K I S
U R K U           S N E L
T C U T           G L E S
```

42. OPEN THE DOOR!

Shaped like a refrigerator, the grid contains things often found in a refrigerator. The hidden message answers the riddle "What's the easiest way to make good food?"

BAKING SODA

BUTTER

CATSUP

CREAM

CRISPER

EGG TRAY

ICE CUBES

JELLY

LEFTOVERS

MAYONNAISE

MEAT

MILK

MUSTARD

ORANGE JUICE

SALAD DRESSING

SHELVES

TOMATO

TUPPERWARE

TV DINNER

YOGURT

```
C T U P P E R W A R E
P H A N S M I L K G S
U E M Y A R T G G E I
S S H E L V E S T C A
T   R   A   H   E   N
A C B E D T M C C F N
C S A I D R U R I S O
R R K T R B S E U   Y
I E I L E E T T J   A
S V N S S T A T E   M
P O G N S T R U G O Y
E T S T I E D B N R L
R F O I N D N G A O L
O E D D G T V O R A E
N L A T O M A T O F J
```

43. SEA HERE!

Every item in the word list contains the letters SEA in consecutive order. When these letters appear in the sea-horse-shaped grid, they have been replaced by a ⌒ (sea wave). So, for example, the phrase ARRIVES EARLY in the list would appear as ARRIVE⌒RLY in the grid. The hidden message completes this statement: "For gamblers in a movie about a famous racehorse, it was hard to…"

BACK SEAT

INSEAM

"IT'S EASY!"

"LET'S EAT!"

RED SEA

RISE AND SHINE

SEA BASS

SEABED

SEA DEVIL

SEA LEVEL

SEALING UP

SEANCE

SEAN PENN

SEARCH

SEASHORE

SEAT BELT

SEATTLE

SEAWEED

TEN CENTS EACH

WISEACRE

```
        ~ I L ~
      O N B N ~ D B
    T ~ K C A B E E
    M ~ E   ~ S H O R E
    T T T       O S
    N B D E
~       E ~ N L
  N B L I I E
  ~ P T T H V
  B ~ E E S E
  S I P N D L
Y     U C N ~
    ~ G E ~ S
    W N N I
    E I T R       C E
    E L ~ U     I     L
    D ~ C C         T
      T H ~ R C H T
        L I V E D ~
```

44. ZIP IT UP

Shaped like zipper latch and part of a zipper, the grid contains things that often have a zipper. The hidden message poses the question "If you have to dress right to follow a dress code, do you have to..."

BACKPACK	LUGGAGE
BOOTS	PANTS
DRESS	PARKA
GOWN	PURSES
GYM BAG	SKIRT
JACKET	SLEEPING BAG
KEY CASE	TENT
LINING	TOTES

```
S                                    J
  T                               A
    O                         C
      O           L           K
  G A B G N I P E E L S
  Z I N Y P N R T D I T
  L G W M   I   H R N T
    U O B   N   T E O
    F G A   G   T S O
      L G       L S
        O A W A K
        T Z G I E
        K O R E Y
        C T T I C
        A P C E A
        P A N T S
        K       E
        C       S
        A       R
        B O D E U
        A K R A P
```

45. GET IT WHITE

Shaped like a castle in chess (a game in which half the pieces are white), the grid contains things that are always or often white. The hidden message answers the riddle "What did Santa say when he disagreed with the weather forecast for no snow on Christmas?"

CHALK	POLAR BEAR
CLOUD	RICE
COTTON	SNOW
LILY	SWAN
LINEN	TEETH
MILK	UNDERWEAR
NOISE	UNICORN
ONION	VANILLA [ICE CREAM]
PEARL	[THE] WHITE HOUSE

```
P  I     E  T  W        Y  S
G  E  N  O  C  H  L     N  N
A  T  A  L  L  I  N  A  V
      W  R  L  T  R
      S  U  L  E  R
      K  L  A  H  C
      N  O  K  O  U
      C  L  O  U  D
      I  O  N  S  T
   M  N  I  T  E  S  T
   N  C  O  E  T  N  A
   O  L  T  I  L  O  I
   R  I  H  W  H  S  W  N  L
N  U  N  D  E  R  W  E  A  R  I
T  P  O  L  A  R  B  E  A  R  E
```

46. A THIRST FOR WORDS

Shaped like a drinking glass, the grid contains beverages kids like to drink. The hidden message is a punny statement about a certain kind of athlete.

COKE	NECTAR
DR PEPPER	PEPSI
EGGNOG	ROOT BEER
EVIAN	SEVEN-UP
GRAPE JUICE	SMOOTHIE
HOT COCOA	SNAPPLE
ICED TEA	SODA
LEMONADE	TANG
MILK SHAKE	WATER

```
A   B   S   O   W   E   V   I   A   N   X
L   E   M   O   N   A   D   E   E   R   G
S   A   O   C   O   C   T   O   H   O   F
A   V   O   O   R   D   A   E   N   I   T
R   A   T   C   E   N   N   G   R   S   E
    D   H   C   R   R   G   I   O   N
    K   I   I   S   E   R   D   P   I
        E   L   P   P   A   N   S
            U   U   P   P   P
            N   E   E
            E   P   J
            V   R   U
            E   D   I
            S   N   C
            C   O   E
    M   I   L   K   S   H   A   K   E
    R   E   E   B   T   O   O   R   H
```

47. Y NOT?

The Y-shaped grid contains things starting with the letter Y. The hidden message is a famous Y-word from the world of cartoons.

YACHT	YESTERDAY
YAHOO	YETI
YAHTZEE	YIELD
YAKKETY-YAK	"YIKES!"
YALE	YMCA
YANKEES	YODEL
YAO MING	YOGA
YARDS	YOLK
YARMULKE	YO-YO
YAWN	YUCKY
YEAH	YUKON
YEAST	YUMMY
YELLOWSTONE	

```
N Y Y                     Y A A
W B S A                 A Y B G
A Y E A H             R A E N O
Y U K O N O       D L E I Y Y
  A I T E Y O   S E Z M D Y
  Y E L L O W S T O N E
  O A Y Y B H A T S
  L A O A Y S T
  K Y L A E
  K B E R E
  E Y D M K
  T A O U N
  Y A Y L A
  Y U C K Y
  A M M E D
  K O C M O
  T H C A Y
```

48. PUT ON A HAPPY FACE

Shaped like a smiley face, the grid contains words and phrases associated with happiness and a positive attitude.

AT EASE

"BE HAPPY"

CALM

CHEERY

CONFIDENT

"DON'T WORRY"

EAGER

ELATED

GLAD

"[THE] GLASS IS HALF FULL"

"GREAT!"

GRIN

"HAVE A NICE DAY"

IN A GOOD

MOOD

JOLLY

JOYFUL

MERRY

OPTIMISTIC

PHAT

ROSY

SERENE

SMILE

SUNNY

THUMBS-UP

UPBEAT

```
        O  L  I  D  T  M
     O  T  U  P  B  E  A  T  E  U
  B  T  F  H  T  T  C  H  E  E  R  Y
  C  H  Y  ●  U  E  I  P  ●  S  R  A
  Y  O  N     I  M  N  M     G  E  Y
H  J  A  N  P  P  Y  L  B  A  I  S  A  G  L  C
S  L  L  U  F  F  L  A  H  S  I  S  S  A  L  G
M  E  L  S  A  I  M  C  A  P  U  P  T  E  O  R
I  N  A  G  O  O  D  M  O  O  D  P  L  I  J  E
L  E  I  R  R  B  E  H  A  P  P  Y  C  A
E  R  E  O  I  E  S  N  T  O  A  C  G  T
   E  L  S  A  N  M  I  T  N  C  L  H
   S  Y  O  A           W  A  D  E
   H  A  V  E  A  N  I  C  E  D  A  Y
   D  O  N  T  W  O  R  R  Y  R
      E  L  A  T  E  D
```

49. OPEN FOR BUSINESS

Shaped like a can of worms, the grid contains things you open. To open a can of worms is to bring up something that is best left unsaid. The hidden message answers the question "Who should be the only ones to open a can of worms?"

BOOK	[YOUR] EYES	[AN] OLD WOUND
BOXES	FILE	PRESENT
CAGE	GATE	PURSE
CARD	JACKET	SAFE
CLASP	JARS	SUITCASE
CRATE	LOCK	TREASURE CHEST
DOOR	[YOUR] MIND	UMBRELLA
ENVELOPE	[YOUR] MOUTH	WINDOW

```
            P                         E   D

         O  C  A  R  D                O

                  N        T  O  P              L

   C  L  A  S  P           U     R            E

   R           R           O     E     E  T  A  G

   A           E           W     A     F

   T     K  W  S  H  O  D  L  S  O  A  N

   E     O  E  E  D  E  L  P  U  R  S  E

         O  D  N  B  E  O  M  R  E  A  A

         B  I  T  R  F  O  I  E  G  T  J

         W  O  B  S  U  I  T  C  A  S  E

         F  M  X  T  S  L  L  H  C  D  O

         U  R  H  E  P  O  L  E  V  N  E

         F  I  Y  S  S  C  H  S  I  I  N

            E  J  A  C  K  E  T  G  M
```

50. WHAT AN ICE GAME

Shaped like a hockey goalie, the grid contains words and phrases about hockey. The hidden message is a scary fact about the early decades of the sport.

ASSIST	PUCK
BENCH	RINK
BLADE	SAVE
DEFENSEMAN	SHOT
GOAL	SKATE
HAT TRICK	STANLEY CUP
ICING	STICK
LINE	WHISTLE
MASK	WING
PASS	ZAMBONI
PERIOD	ZONE

```
            K K I
            N C T
          H I I E
            N R T G R S
          G O S S H O T
        E N I L A L D A T
  I       E S Z A M B O N I A D
    D   S S I D A L W I L   N H T
      E T A K S S A H I R E   W E A
      F V   K D I   N E Y
      R E   E S A   G P C
        N T S       F U H
        L S A       C P C
      E A E E       M N K
      P O A   M     S E K
        G       A       B
            E N O Z
```

51. PLUG IT IN

Shaped like a plug, the grid contains things you plug in. The hidden message answers the riddle "What happened to the boy who got it backwards when he was told to take a little plug?"

AMPS	MICROPHONE
CLOCK	MICROWAVE
COMPUTER	MODEM
CORD	PRINTER
DRYER	STEREO
FANS	TOASTER
IRON	TV SET
LAMP	WASHER

```
        H N D
        E R O
      T Y E O R
    T E S V T E I
    R O P A K T A
  P E S M W B N I C
  M N G A O G I O L
  A O S U R L R E O
F L H D P C D P R C I
N E P S E I T E E K A
R D O C O M P U T E R
    R             S
    C             A
    I             O
    M             T
```

52. I NEED THIS RIDE NOW!

Shaped like a horse, the grid contains things you ride, ride in, or ride on. The hidden message is something you ride that takes you right back to where you started.

BIKE	PONY
BOAT	SCOOTER
BUSES	SLED
CAMEL	SLEIGH
FERRIS WHEEL	SUBWAY
JETS	TAXI
LIMO	TROLLEY
LUGE	VANS
MONORAIL	WAGON

```
        P A M
      F R O O
  C A M E L N N
      O L R O Y
        O G R L
      I A M A I
      W X E I V S
      R B A L L A W
  S C O O T E R N H C
  T       Y A W B U S E S
  E             T R O L L E Y
  J             O A E K     L
    S           D I         U
                B G         G
                T H         E
            E R
```

111

53. NEW YORK, NEW YORK

Shaped like the top part of the Empire State Building, the grid contains words and phrases associated with New York City. The hidden message is a fact that begins "Because New York has so much going on all of the time..."

BROADWAY

BRONX ZOO

BUSES

CENTRAL PARK

DELI

FASHION

FERRY

HARLEM

MACY'S

MUSEUMS

OPERA

PIZZA

SAKS

SKYSCRAPERS

SOHO

STATUE OF LIBERTY

SUBWAY

TAXI

TIMES SQUARE

WALL STREET

```
                  Y
                  T
                  R
                  E
                  B
              I   I M
          B   I   L E D
      S   T   R   F L T E
      C   E   S   O R R S
  S   C   O   E   S E A M U M F
  O   K   N   R   N U H D B L E
  S   M   A   T   Q T B Y W C R
  Y   U   A   S   L A R L A A R
  C   S   S   L   E T D A Y T Y
I H A E E L C S I P L O H O S
X T M U F A S H I O N P Y P T
A I H M A W T Z N E V E A E R
T S L S E E Z O O Z X N O R B
P S R E P A R C S Y K S S A K
```

54. AW, NUTS!

Every item in the word list contains the letters NUT in consecutive order. When these letters appear in the acorn-shaped grid, they have been replaced by a 🌰. We hope this puzzle doesn't drive you 🌰S. The hidden message completes the sentence "Nuts are often a healthy food, so..."

BRAZIL NUT

BUTTERNUT SQUASH

CHESTNUT

COCONUT

DIMINUTIVE

DONUTS

HAZELNUT

IN A NUTSHELL

LAST-MINUTE

LUG NUT

MR. PEANUT

NUT-BROWN

NUTCASE

"[THE] NUTCRACKER"

NUTMEG

NUTRITION

NUTS AND BOLTS

"[THE] NUTTY PROFESSOR"

ROASTED NUTS

WALNUT

```
                    H
🌰 🌰  S  🌰  D  E  T  S  A  O  R  L  I  T  B
S  T  L  O  B  D  N  A  S  🌰  L  M  H  R  A
   K  Y  A  E  S  S  U  E  E  E  N  A  S
      E  P  W  T  H  Q  H  A  V  Z  Z
   🌰  N  R  L  A  S  T  M  I  🌰  E
      C  O  C  O  🌰  🌰  T  L  🌰  C  L
      A  I  N  A  F  R  🌰  U  I  R  🌰
      S  T  N  🌰  A  E  P  R  M  A  T
      E  I  I  G  S  T  S  I  I  C  N
      N  R  U  U  T  T  R  S  D  K  G
      🌰  I  L  T  U  I  O  O  E
      N  W  O  R  B  🌰  O  M  R
         C  H  E  S  T  🌰  U
                  S
```

55. LOSER!

Shaped like a key, the grid contains things you might lose. The hidden message answers the riddle "What happened to the boy who got bored and took all the money out of his savings account?"

A BET	KEYS
CASH	[YOUR] MIND
COMB	POWER
FAITH	PRIVILEGES
GAME	[YOUR] TEMPER
GLASSES	TIME
[YOUR] GRIP	TRUST
[YOUR] HOMEWORK	[YOUR] TURN
HOPE	WEIGHT

```
          E  M  A  G
       T  U  R  N  L  C
 H  I  E           A  O  L
 W  M  P  P  F  S  M  A
 O  E  R  I  A  S  B  C
 D  S  I  R  I  E  A  R
    N  V  G  T  S  E
    I  T  H  W
    L  M  O  T
 R  E  P  M  E  T
    G  I  N  S
    E  K  U
    S  R
    T  O  T
    E  W
    K  E  Y  S
    R  M  E
    H  O  P  E
    S  H  T
```

56. GET A LOAD OF THIS!

Shaped like a rocket ship, the grid carries a full payload of 25 items—24 in the word list and one in the hidden message. Each item is made from letters that appear in the phrase ROCKET SHIP. (Note: no letter is ever repeated within a word.) When you're done with the puzzle, try a different game: see how many more words you can make from the letters in ROCKET SHIP. One final thought…in the hidden message, the ROCKET SHIP turns into a certain make of car.

CHIP	OSTRICH	SHOCK
CHOIR	PITCHERS	SHREK
CHOKE	PITH	SICKER
CREST	POETIC	SKETCH
ECHO	POKER	SPORT
ESCORT	PORCH	TREK
HEROIC	RICHEST	TRICEPS
HORSE	ROCKIEST	TROPHIES

```
              R
           E  E  P
           S  K  O
        T  R  O  P  S
        T  O  P  O  E
        S  H  R  E  K
        E  H  I  T  O
        I  C  O  I  H
        K  R  H  C  C
        C  T  C  O  K
        O  T  R  C  P
        R  S  R  I  S
        I  H  T  O  C
     C  C  C  R  R  P  E
  K  T  H  R  O  E  I  H  P
E  E  E  E  O  C  H  T  C  I  S
R  K  R     S  P  S  C  H     H  E  H
S  S  T     T  S  E  R  C     C  E  S
```

Shaped like a bell, the grid contains things you hear or listen to. The hidden message completes the joke "Do you know that the smartest kid in class is going deaf?"

ANNOUNCEMENT	PLEA
BARK	RUMOR
BELL	SCREAM
"DUCK!"	SHOUT
ENGINE	SIREN
EXCUSE	SONG
"FIRE!"	TEACHER
HONK	THUNDER
[YOUR] MOTHER	VERDICT
"OOPS!"	"YOU'VE GOT MAIL!"

```
                  R
                  E
                  H
            H  O  C  U  H
         I  N  B  A  R  K  V
         K  S  B  E  L  L  E
         C  M  O  T  H  E  R
         U  C  A  N  R  E  D
         D  O  R  E  G  S  I
      T  U  U  D  M  R  U  C  P
      U  M  N  L  E  O  C  T  L
      O  U  D  R  C  O  X  S  E
   R  H  N  I  T  N  P  E  N  A  H
   T  S  F  E  A  U  S  I  R  E  N
R  L  I  A  M  T  O  G  E  V  U  O  Y
                  N
               E  N  Y
               O  A  U
```

58. ON THE GO

Shaped like a beach umbrella, the grid contains places and things you might go to. The hidden message tells what could happen to you in a game of Monopoly.

AIRPORT

BALL GAME

BEACH

CHURCH

CLASS

DISNEY WORLD

JAIL

MALL

MOVIES

PARK

PARTY

PIECES

ROCK CONCERT

[YOUR] ROOM

SCHOOL

SLEEP

STORE

TOWN

```
                  M
            P  P  Y  O  O  P  N
         O  U  A  I  T  O  A  V  M  W  I
         S  R  G  R  E  R  H  S  I  T  O
      G  T  R  O  C  K  C  O  N  C  E  R  T
      Y  O  P  S  S  L  E  E  P  H  H  S  O
   L  D  R  I  S  L  R  D  E  S  U  C  O  C  T
   I  I  E  M  A  G  L  L  A  B  R  L  A  O  Y
A  T     M  L  O        R     G  C  O     E  L
J           C           O           H        B
                        W
                        Y
                        E
                        N
                        S
                        I
                        D
```

59. SOFT IN THE HEAD

Shaped like a teddy bear, the grid contains things that are or may be soft. The hidden message tells you the famous person for whom the teddy bear was named.

ANGORA

BLANKET

COAL

COTTON

DATA

FOCUS

GLOW

HAIR

JOBS

KISS

LANDING

PILLOW

RABBIT'S FOOT

RAIN

SKIN

SLOPE

SOAP

SPOT

TEDDY BEAR

WATER

```
            P  R  E
         G  N  I  D  N  A  L
         S  I  ●  I  ●  T  L
         S  K  ●  E  A
         S  U  D  O  D
         D  C  S
         R  Y  D  O  O  L  W  E
   R  A  B  B  I  T  S  F  O  O  T
N  I  E     W  A  T  E  R     P  L  T
N  A        O  A  O  T  E     D  E  G
R  H     B  L  A  N  K  E  T
         J  L  D  T  G  Y  R
         O  I  O  P  A  O  S
   O  O  B  P           S  R  E  V
   K  I  S  S           E  L  A  T
```

125

60. FLOATING AWAY

Shaped like a person windsurfing, the grid contains things that float on water. The hidden message completes the riddle "Why did the boy put a canned soft drink in the bathtub with him?" "He wanted…"

ALGAE	LILY PAD
BEACHBALL	LOGS
BUOYS	MARSHMALLOWS
CANOE	MINE
CORK	OIL SLICK
FLOTSAM	OTTER
ICEBERG	PENGUIN
INNER TUBE	RAFT
JELLYFISH	SEAL
KAYAK	SPONGE
LIFE PRESERVER	SWAN

```
                        K
                        T   A
                        O   B   Y   E
        H   L   A       E   O   N   A   C
        V   I   E           A   R   I   A   F   K   N
        L           C       M   A   R   L   C   I   B
        E   Y   E   H       O   A   O   F   O   I   U   U
    J   A   P   B       O       R   O   I   T   L   G   O
    E   G   A   U   T           S   K   C   S   S   N   Y
    L   L   D   T               H   S   E   A   L   E   S
    L   A   E   R               M   T   B   M   I   P   N
    Y   R   B   E               A   E   E   E   O   A
    F           N               L   R   R   N   W
    I           N               L   O   G   S
    S           I               O   E
    H   F       L   O           W
A   L   I   F   E   P   R   E   S   E   R   V   E   R   T
```

61. IT'S A GIFT!

Shaped like a party balloon, the grid contains things kids
might like to get for birthday gifts. The hidden message is a
definition of a gifted child.

BMX BIKE
BOOK
BRACELET
CAMCORDER
CELLPHONE
CHARM
CLOTHES
DOLL
DVDS

GAMEBOY
LAPTOP
MONEY
ROLLERBLADES
SHOES
STEREO
TV SET
VIDEOGAME
WALKMAN

```
        A M K I D
      W O E R E T S
    C N A M K L A W H
  C E K I B X M B O G E
  Y L R E D R O C M A C
  T L O S B O O K A L O
  T P L T E L E C A R B
  O H T O H L A P T O P
  F O V I D E O G A M E
  P N S R E R S E O H S
    E E Y O B E M A G
      T S E L N T S
        C H A R M
            D
            E
            S
      D
    V
  D
```

62. PUT YOUR HOUSE IN ORDER

Here are the HOUSE RULES. Every item in the word list contains the letters HOUSE in consecutive order. When these letters appear in the house-shaped grid, they have been replaced by a 🏠. So make a 🏠 PARTY out of this 🏠 WORK because this puzzle is ON THE 🏠.

BOATHOUSE

CLEAN HOUSE

CLUBHOUSE

COURTHOUSE

DOGHOUSE

DOLLHOUSE

FARMHOUSE

FIREHOUSE

GREENHOUSE
 EFFECT

HOTHOUSE

HOUSECOAT

HOUSEFLY

HOUSEHOLD

HOUSEKEEPER

HOUSE OF CARDS

HOUSE OF
 COMMONS

HOUSE-SITS

[THE] HOUSE
 THAT JACK BUILT

HOUSE-TO-
 HOUSE SURVEY

HOUSEWARMING

HOUSEWIFE

JAILHOUSE

LIGHTHOUSE

OPEN HOUSE

OUTHOUSE

PENTHOUSE

ROUGHHOUSE

SPEAKER OF
 THE HOUSE

TOLLHOUSE
 COOKIES

TREE HOUSE

```
                    A
              🏠  🏠  D      B  🏠
           H  O  T  🏠  L  H  🏠
           D  R  O  K  U  G  O  T
        O  E  🏠  T  R  U  O  C  H
        G  N  R  D  B  O  A  T  🏠  A  🏠
     🏠  N  Y  E  V  R  U  S  🏠  O  T  🏠  🏠
        L  I  O  P  E  N  🏠  L  🏠  O  J  N  O
        I  M  🏠  E  G  B  🏠  E  C  E  A  🏠  F
        G  R  E  E  N  🏠  E  F  F  E  C  T  C
        H  A  R  K  R  R  O  I  L  K  K  N  A
        T  W  I  🏠  T  🏠  W  C  J  Y  B  E  R
     🏠  🏠  F  E  L  🏠  I  🏠  N  A  U  P  D
        T  T  O  L  L  🏠  C  O  O  K  I  E  S
        S  N  O  M  M  O  C  F  O  🏠  L  L  O
        A  D  🏠  F  A  R  M  🏠  S  I  T  S  🏠
     🏠  E  H  T  F  O  R  E  K  A  E  P  S
```

63. TAKE FIVE

Shaped like the number 5, the grid contains 23 five-letter words that each begin with a different letter of the alphabet. The hidden message answers the question "So who's missing?"

AGENT	NOISY
BLAZE	OWING
CENTS	PRIDE
DRINK	QUIET
ELBOW	RAISE
FENCE	SCENT
HELLO	TENSE
IGLOO	VEXED
JOUST	WINGS
KNIFE	X-RAYS
LIMBO	ZEBRA
MIXED	

```
H  E  L  L  O  B  M  I  L  O
E  L  B  O  W  I  N  G  S  H
E  A  L
F  G  T
I  E  E
N  N  N
K  T  S  C  E  N  T  S
S  V  E  X  E  D  R  I  N  K
            A  O  O  Q
            I  T  U
            S  S  I
            Y  U  E
M  E  G        A  U  O  T
B  L  A  Z  E  B  R  A  Y  J
P  R  I  D  E  X  I  M
```

64. GET INTO SHAPE

Shaped like a parallelogram, the grid contains the names of distinctive shapes found in math and elsewhere. The hidden message answers the riddle "The name of which famous New York City place is made up of an arithmetic term and shape?"

CIRCLE	PRISM
CONE	RECTANGLE
CROSS	SPHERE
CYLINDER	SPIRAL
DONUT	SQUARE
HELIX	STAR
OCTAGON	TRAPEZOID
OVAL	TRIANGLE

```
                        E
                     L  R
                  C  E  A
                  R  C  L  U
               I  T  O  G  Q
            C  A  C  N  N  S
         T  N  R  I  E  A  M
      E  G  O  H  E  L  I  X
   M  L  S  S  S  T  A  R  S
O  E  S  P  H  E  R  E  T
C  Y  L  I  N  D  E  R
T  D  Q  R  R  U  A
A  O  V  A  L  P
G  N  A  L  E
O  U  R  Z
N  T  O
E  I
D
```

65. IT LOOKS LIKE REIGN

Shaped like a king in chess, the grid contains words and phrases associated with royalty. The hidden message answers the riddle "Why is a king like a 12-inch measuring tool found in a classroom?"

CASTLE

COURT

CROWN

DUCHESS

EARL

HER MAJESTY

KING

MONARCH

PALACE

PRINCE

QUEEN

REALM

ROBE

ROYALS

THRONE

TIARA

```
            E
        K   T   A
            I
    H C R A N O M
        C N R H G
        R E A L M
        E   I   T
  S A D U C H E S S
        Q   P   R
        E   R   O
        L   I   N
        T   N   E
        S   C   B
        A   E   O
        L C R R U
      A C R O W N R
  U P L S L A Y O R T E
  H E R M A J E S T Y R
```

66. JUST DESERTS

Shaped like a saguaro cactus, the grid contains things associated with deserts. The hidden message is the punch line to a joke that begins "How was your family's day trip to the desert?"

ALOE	HEAT
ARID	LAWRENCE OF ARABIA
ARROYO	MESAS
BEDOUIN	MOJAVE
BUTTE	OASIS
CACTUS	RATTLESNAKE
CAMEL	ROCKS
CANYON	SAGUARO
CARAVAN	SAHARA
COYOTE	SALT LAKE
DEATH VALLEY	SAND
GOBI	SCORPION

```
          M Y D S
        D H A I D L
  I B   K E S R S C
  E E   S A H A R A        S C
  M D   O T G T D N        U A
  I O T B U T T E Y        T M
  B U J A U T L I O    D I C E
A I B A R A F O E C N E R W A L
  N D O V N D T S T E H I N C
    K I E E N N T K S W A
        N A V A R A C S
        O T S K S L
        I H O E K T
        P V M T C L
        R A H O O A
        O L E Y R S
        C L G O B I
        S E O C L T
        O Y O R R A
```

67. CLOWNING AROUND

Shaped like a person on stilts, the grid contains things associated with a circus. The hidden message names a performer you'll never see in a circus...his act of dominating a certain lawn weed is just too mild.

ACROBAT	HIGH WIRE
BALLOONS	HORSES
BAND	LION
BARNUM	RINGS
BIG TOP	STILT
CLOWN	TENT
ELEPHANTS	TRAPEZE

```
        D S A
        P   N
        O
        T O T
      E H L A G
    N W O L C D I
  T     R A R       B
  R     S B         A
  A     E E         R
  P   B S S A N     N
  E   A G   T O     U
  Z   N     I       M
  E I D     L L     S
  R L       I I     T
  I O N     T A     N
  W                 A
  H                 H
  G                 P
  I                 E
  H                 L
  M                 E
  E                 R
```

68. IT ALL ADDS UP

Shaped like a protractor, the grid contains math and arithmetic words. The hidden message answers the riddle "What do you say to a kid who needs a hint on an addition problem?"

ADDS

ANGLE

AREA

AXIS

DIAMETER

DIVIDE

HYPOTENUSE

LINE

MATH

MATRIX

MINUS

NUMBERS

PRODUCT

QUOTIENT

RADIUS

ROOT

TOTAL

ZERO

```
            O  C  A  N
         I  G  R  R  I  N  V  S
      E  T  N  E  I  T  O  U  Q  I
   R  O  O  T  Z        Y  X  M  O  X
   R  T  U  E                 I  B  S  A
   A  U  M                    R  E  E
L  D  A  M        L  A        H  T  R  H
E  I  L     D  I  V  I  D  E     T  A  S
D  U  E  L  G  N  A  P  R  O  D  U  C  T  A  M
E  S  U  N  E  T  O  P  Y  H  P  S  U  N  I  M
```

69. THE WHEEL THING

Shaped like a bicycle, the grid contains words about cycling. The hidden message answers the riddle "What did the exhausted boy say after changing both flats on his bike?"

BELL	RACE
FALL	RIDE
FLAT	RIMS
LANE	SEAT
PATCH	TIRE
PATH	TUBE
PEDALS	WHEEL
PUMP	

```
   I
   F A L L         W H E E L
   A                   R
   N P A T C H       I T
   E                 T
      D     C      M     A
L  A          A    T     P  I
F  L  A  T       R  I  D  E  B  U  T  R
S  E  A  T                S  M  I  R
B  E                      P  D
```

70. PRETTY CHEESY

Shaped like a piece of Swiss cheese, the grid contains the names of different cheeses. The hidden message asks a question about a certain TV celebrity.

BLUE	HAVARTI
BRIE	MONTEREY JACK
CHEDDAR	MOZZARELLA
COLBY	MUENSTER
EDAM	PARMESAN
FETA	PROVOLONE
FONTINA	RICOTTA
GOAT CHEESE	ROMANO
GORGONZOLA	SWISS
GOUDA	VELVEETA

```
I  A  L  L  E  R  A  Z  Z  O  M
M  U  E  N  S  T  E  R  S     S  H
T  P  A  N  E  Y           R  A
M  A  R  F  O  B           A  V
O  R  Y  V  E  L  V  E  E  T  A
N  M        R  O  O  O  A  M  R
T  E        C  C  A  V  L  N  T
E  S  E  E  H  C  T  A  O  G  I
R  A  M  O  E  B        Z  R  A
E  N  B  A  D  L        N  R  P
Y  I  G  A  D  U  O  G  O  S  C
J        A  E  H  M  G  W  E
A        R  E  A  B  R  I  E
C  A  N  I  T  N  O  F  O  S  S
K  A  T  T  O  C  I  R  G  S  E
```

71. I'D LIKE TO POINT OUT...

Shaped like an arrow, the grid contains things that have points. The hidden message answers the riddle "What did the female fencer say to her opponent as she jabbed him with her sword?"

ANTLERS

ARGUMENT

ARROW

BARBED WIRE

BAYONET

DART

FANG

FISHHOOK

GOLF TEE

KNIFE

NAILS

NEEDLE

PENCILS

PINS

QUILL

SKI POLE

SPEAR

STINGER

TACK

UNICORN'S HORN

```
            P  E  N  C  I  L  S
            E  N  S  P  H  K  E
            R  E  L  L  I  U  Q
            I  E  S  P  A  N  I
            W  D  O  D  D  I  S
            D  L  S  T  A  C  K
            E  E  T  F  L  O  G
            B  B  I  I  N  R  D
            R  A  N  F  A  N  G
   W  O  R  R  A  Y  G  F  I  S  H  H  O  O  K
      A  Y  R  B  O  E  O  L  H  U  D  G  N
         N  E  A  N  R  T  S  O  A  M  I
            T  N  E  M  U  G  R  A  F
            L  T  P  Y  T  N  E
            E  P  S  O  I
            R  N  T
            S
```

72. SOMETHING IS FISHY

Shaped like a lobster, the grid contains things that live in the water. The hidden message answers the riddle "What did the kid at the seashore want on his sandwich?"

CARP

CLAM

CORAL

CRAB

DOLPHIN

ELECTRIC EEL

HAMMERHEAD SHARK

KELP

LOBSTER

MUSSEL

OCTOPUS

OYSTER

PIRANHA

PORPOISE

SCALLOP

SEAL

SKATE

SNAIL

SNAPPER

SQUID

TURTLE

WHALE

```
          P  L     C  E
          T  I  A     N  O  S
       U  A  U           K  R  T
       N  B     R  U  A     T  A
    S           T  T  P              L
       N        E  O  L           O
 E           A  R  A  Y  E  E  B           N
   O  C  T  O  P  U  S  K  S  Q  U  I  D
             D  P  T  T     I
 M  U  S  S  E  L  I  E  D  O  L  P  H  I  N
             L  R  R  R  P
 K  R  A  H  S  D  A  E  H  R  E  M  M  A  H
 J           E  N  H  P  O              L
             B  H  R  W  P
       L  Y     M  A  L  C  F     I  S
       L  E  E  C  I  R  T  C  E  L  E
       H  P  O  L  L  A  C  S  E  A  L
```

151

73. MAKING DECISIONS

Shaped like a man sticking out his tongue and making a face, the grid contains things you make. The hidden message answers the question "There's a saying, 'Haste makes waste,' but would you say that's true for bank robbers?"

BELIEVE

CONTACT

[A] DETOUR

[A] DIFFERENCE

DINNER

[AN] EXCUSE

[A] FACE

[A] FIRE

[THE] FIRST MOVE

[A] FOOL OF YOURSELF

FRIENDS

[A] FUSS

MATTERS WORSE

MERRY

MONEY

MY DAY

NICE

POPCORN

ROOM

SENSE

[THE] TEAM

TROUBLE

WAVES

YOUR BED

```
                N   Y   O   F   T   I
            F   C   O   N   T   A   C   T
            T   R   O   U   B   L   E   C   T
            H   E   E   R   D   I   N   N   E   R
        F   R   ●   B   S   M   M   Y   C   R
        I   N   ●   E   Y   A   E   A   N   L
    O   F   R   I   E   N   D   S   T   O   K   E   I
    N   G   S   C   S   A   D   E   T   O   U   R   T
        T   E   Y   N   E   V   E   I   L   E   B
        M   T   O   R   M   S   R   M   A   F   K
F   O   O   L   O   F   Y   O   U   R   S   E   L   F   E
        V   A   O   C   Q   U   W   U   I   I   C
        K   E   R   X   P   G   E   O   T   F   D
        A   Y   E   N   O   M   E   R   R   Y
                P   W   A   S   Y
                W   A   V   E   S
```

74. IT'S A PUT-ON

Shaped like a boot, the grid contains things associated with shoes. The hidden message is good advice from a music teacher.

BALLET SLIPPERS
BLISTERS
CLOGS
CORNS
COWBOY BOOTS
ESPADRILLE
FLATS
GALOSHES
HEELS
LACES
LEATHER
LIFTS
LOAFER

MOCCASINS
MULES
POLISH
PUMP
SANDAL
SHOEHORN
SLIP-ON
SNEAKER
SOLE
STRAP
TASSEL
ZORI

```
                        R   P   L   E   A   Y   S
                        L   E   S   S   A   T   A
                        S   F   F   P   R   R   E
                        R   E   K   A   E   N   S
                        E   N   P   D   O   T   S
                        P   Z   C   R   F   L   N
                        P   O   L   I   S   H   I
                    S   I   R   L   L   T   H   S
                H   L   I   H   L   O   G   A
            H   O   S   O   R   E   O   N   C
        S   R   E   T   S   I   L   B   O   C
    N   P   H   H   E   B   C   S   Y   P   O
S   U   M   T   M   S   N   O   L   L   E       O   I   M
T   O   T   U   O   A   S   R   L   C   S       B   L   H
A   O   P   L   L   A   D   N   A   S           W   S   E
L   E   A   T   H   E   R   L   B               O   E   H
F   G   C   O   R   N   S   O                   C   R   N
```

75. TOTAL ECLIPSE OF THE MOON

The moon-shaped grid was supposed to be filled with words and phrases containing the word MOON, but there's been a total lunar eclipse. As a result, the word MOON, which appears throughout the word list, has completely disappeared from the grid. So, for example, MOONBEAM in the list will appear only as BEAM in the grid. When you're done, the hidden message completes this definition: "The word 'half-moon' can also mean the white part at the…"

CRESCENT
MOON
FULL MOON
HALF-MOON
HARVEST MOON
HONEYMOON

MAN IN THE MOON
MOONBEAM
"MOONLIGHT SONATA"
MOONRAKER
MOONSCAPE
MOONSHINE

MOON SHOT
MOONSTONE
MOONSTRUCK
MOONWALK
"PAPER MOON"

```
            B Y E N O H
          F L A H M A
        A S E T A H
        S T O N E A
        K A I B R
    O L N F V S
    A A O E H
    M W S O P
    F T T I A
    S N H N P
    F H G G E S
        U I E R C
        R L N N A S
          A L E P I E
          L R E K A R
            S T R U C K
```

76. GREENHOUSE

Shaped like a shamrock, the grid houses the names of plants, foods, and other things that are always or often green. The hidden message contains the names of three famous fictional characters with green skin.

ALGAE	LAWN
AVOCADO	LEAF
BEAN	MINT
CACTI	MOSS
CELERY	PEAR
DRAGON	PEAS
EMERALD	PICKLE
GARDENER'S THUMB	PINE
GRAPE	POISON IVY
GRASS	SLIME
JADE	SPINACH

```
            G  M  I
            G  R  N  I  M
            D  R  A  G  O  N  C
            R  A  S  S  E  D  T
            B  P  S  Y  I  B  L
            E  L  V  E  A
   E  H  P        A  I  W        C  U  A
   L  M  K  Y  E        N        A  K  E  V  R
M  I  E  T  R  T  A        O     C  H  E  E  O  F  L
G  A  R  D  E  N  E  R  S  T  H  U  M  B  C  E  R
O  E  A  G  L  A  G        I     S  P  I  N  A  C  H
A  L  N  E  D        O           G  L  F  D  R
   D  I  C        P              S  N  O
                  E
               N  A  D
               I  C  S  H  A
            P  I  C  K  L  E  J
```

159

77. STRINGS ATTACHED

Shaped like a kite with a tail, the grid contains things with strings. The hidden message answers the riddle "What did the frustrated boy say when he quit tying a string around his finger because it never helped him to remember?"

BALLOONS	MARIONETTE
BANJO	MASK
BEAN	MITTENS
BOWS	PIANO
CAT'S CRADLE	PULL TOY
GUITAR	VIOLIN
HARP	YO-YO
KITE	

```
              O
           N  F  J
        A  O  I  E  N
     I  B  M  M  L  Y  A
  P  R  A  H  A  D  O  K  B
R  S  S  L  G  R  A  T  I  U  G
  K  W  L  E  I  R  L  T  V
     Y  O  Y  O  C  L  E
     T  O  B  N  S  U  I
     N  E  E  T  P
     S  A  T  A  T
     N  T  C
     E
        T
           T
              I
                 M
```

78. PLAYING IT SAFE

Shaped like a shield, the grid contains things that protect in different ways. The hidden message tells something the president of the United States promises to do while taking the oath of office.

ARMOR

BABY BIB

BUG SPRAY

BULLETPROOF VEST

CANDY WRAPPER

COAT

COPS

FENDER

GAS MASK

GLOVES

GOGGLES

GUARD

HELMET

LOCK

MOAT

SAFETY GLASS

SHIELD

TEFLON

VACCINE

WALL

```
G  E  R  P  B  I  B  Y  B  A  B
A  N  E  B  U  G  S  P  R  A  Y
S  I  D  R  L  O  C  M  E  T  E
M  C  N  C  L  T  O  O  P  A  D
A  C  E  T  E  R  N  T  P  R  D
S  A  F  E  T  Y  G  L  A  S  S
K  V  G  M  P  D  O  U  R  O  E
F  T  E  L  R  N  G  D  W  T  M
N  A  H  E  O  L  G  A  Y  E  C
   O  O  H  O  V  L  N  D  S
   C  L  C  F  L  E  T  N  I
      K  F  V  T  S  S  A
      D  L  E  I  H  S  C
         U  S  T  T  I
         T  O  N
```

79. ARE YOU PACKED?

Shaped liked a pull suitcase on wheels, the grid contains things you might pack for a Florida vacation. The hidden message tells you what you should do with both your suitcase and your vacation.

BATHING SUIT	SHORTS
BEACH TOWEL	SOCKS
CAMERA	SUNGLASSES
COMB	SUN HAT
JACKET	SUNSCREEN
MAGAZINES	TANK TOP
MAKEUP	TOOTHBRUSH
MONEY	T-SHIRT
SANDALS	WATCH

```
        B   T       R
        A           Y
        T           W
        H           A
        I           T
T   O   S   U   N   S   C   R   E   E   N
B   M   O   C   G   T   H   P   T   J   S
E   H   A   C   S   M   K   A   A   A   U
A   S   A   H   U   A   N   S   R   C   N
C   U   I   S   I   K   N   M   E   K   G
H   R   M   H   T   E   U   D   M   E   L
T   B   C   O   S   U   N   H   A   T   A
O   H   P   R   N   P   H   I   C   L   S
W   T   N   T   A   E   S   K   C   O   S
E   O   S   S   Y   O   Y   U   C   A   E
L   O   M   A   G   A   Z   I   N   E   S
        T                               N
```

80. I STRAIN

The I-shaped grid contains words and phrases in which I is the only vowel. The hidden message is one critic's opinion of the puzzle. (We hope it's not yours!)

BIG BIRD

BIKINI

CHIP

DIPS

FIGHTING IRISH

FIRST INNING

HISS

ICING

JINX

KILT

LIPSTICK

MISSISSIPPI

NIGHT SHIFT

NITWIT

PICNIC

PRISM

SKIM MILK

SKINTIGHT

SPILL

STRICT

THICK

TWIN

VISIT

WIND CHILL

ZINC

```
M  I  S  S  I  S  S  I  P  P  I  H  C
F  I  R  S  T  I  N  N  I  N  G  I  T
B  I  G  B  I  R  D  J  I  N  X  H  I
         W  H  I  K  I
         T  H  I  C  K
         I  B  I  I  T
         N  I  W  T  N
         P  R  I  S  M
         I  D  I  P  S
         C  T  L  I  K
         N  N  V  L  I
         I  K  I  L  N
         C  M  S  Z  T
         M  I  I  T  I
S  T  F  I  H  S  T  H  G  I  N  T  I
N  K  K  W  I  N  D  C  H  I  L  L  S
H  S  I  R  I  G  N  I  T  H  G  I  F
```

81. WALL-DONE

Shaped like a mirror, the grid contains things you might find on a wall. The hidden message is a comment about Humpty Dumpty.

CALENDAR	PAINT
CHIMES	PENNANT
CLOCKS	PICTURES
DIRT	PLAQUE
EXIT SIGN	POSTER
FLIES	SHELVES
LIGHT SWITCH	SPIDER-MAN
MURAL	THERMOMETER
NAILS	TILES
OUTLET	WALLPAPER

```
            S H T
          L P H H U
        I F L I E S M
      A H P A T R L Y W
  N A C S Q N M T V S W
  E D T I U R O D B E U
  S P I D E R M A N M S
  K I W R T E E H G I E
  C C S O T P T T I H L
  O T T U C A E E S C I
  L U H T A P R W T O T
  C R G L L L T N I A P
  A E I E E L S O X F F
    S L T N A N N E P
      T H D W E W A
        L A R U M
          R L L
```

82. HOW DOES YOUR GARDEN GROW?

Shaped like a watering can, the grid contains things that grow in gardens. The hidden message is a plea to a security guard from would-be shoppers at a gardening store right at closing time.

ASPARAGUS

BEAN

BEET

CARROT

CAULIFLOWER

CELERY

CHARD

EGGPLANT

KALE

LEEK

OKRA

ONION

PARSLEY

PARSNIP

PEAS

POTATO

PUMPKIN

RADISH

ROSEMARY

SAGE

SQUASH

TOMATO

YAMS

ZUCCHINI

```
  I  F                 B  Y  Y  O
U  C  Y  A           R  H  E  R  R  C
C  H  A  R  D        A  S  P  A  R  A  G  U  S
O  T  M  A  E  S     T  I  L  M  N  U           A
L  S        L  Q  Z  O  D  K  E  E  L  P        E
            E  U  M  A  P  S  L  I  U        P
            C  A  R  R  O  T  F  M  P  E
            O  C  T  S  K  R  N  L  P  A
            T  H  O  R  H  B  A  O  K  R
            A  I  A  S  E  E  E  W  I  S
            L  T  N  A  L  P  G  G  E  N  N  E
            T  O  I  A  T  U  C  A  R  T  I  O
            E  P  K  I  Y  E  L  S  R  A  P  N
```

83. BACK TO THE DRAWING BOARD

Shaped like a canvas on an easel, the grid contains things you draw. The hidden message answers the riddle "Why was the female gunslinger good at art?"

A MAP

AWAY

[A] BASE ON BALLS

[A] BATH

[A] BLANK

CARDS

[A] CARTOON

CHEERS

[A] CIRCLE

[A] CONCLUSION

[A] CROWD

[THE] CURTAINS

[A] DEEP BREATH

ENEMY FIRE

[A] HOPSCOTCH AREA

LOTS

NEAR

[AN] OUTLINE

[A] PICTURE

[A] SALARY

STRAWS

[A] SWORD

```
Y  B  E  S  T  R  A  W  S  C  D  A  U
K  A  S  N  E  R  I  F  Y  M  E  N  E
N  E  W  I  O  U  T  L  I  N  E  S  C
A  E  R  A  H  C  T  O  C  S  P  O  H
L  H  A  T  D  R  N  E  I  A  B  W  E
B  C  A  R  T  O  O  N  R  L  R  A  E
S  Q  O  U  U  W  I  I  C  A  E  D  R
C  W  K  C  O  D  S  N  L  R  A  T  S
S  H  P  I  C  T  U  R  E  Y  T  E  D
   A           L           H
   M           C           R
   B  A  S  E  O  N  B  A  L  L  S
   A  A        O           W
   T           C           T
   H                       O
                           L
```

84. PANDEMONIUM

Every item in the word list contains the letters PAN in consecutive order. When these letters appear in the dustpan-shaped grid, they have been replaced by a ☞, so whatever you do, don't ☞ IC! The hidden message tells what some people with strange tastes might like to eat for breakfast.

CHIMPANZEE

COMPANION

DUSTPAN

FLASH IN THE PAN

FRYPAN

GIANT PANDA

HISPANIC

JAPANESE

PANAMA CANAL

PANCAKE

PANELS

PANIC BUTTON

PANORAMA

PANSIES

PINK PANTHER

PROPANE

SMARTY-PANTS

SPANDEX

TIMPANI

WINDOWPANE

S G

M I

A A

R N

T T

Y

C S S D E X I

O J T A E D I

S M A P S M U S H

O I M R W I S A E L

E E I N O T T U B C I

S S O D S T A I A S

E A N N D E S L K O N M

C H I M Z E E E M S A Y A

R Z W I R E H T K N I P R L

A M A R O E H T N I H S A L F

85. ALL SMALL

Shaped like a magnifying glass, the grid contains things that are always or often small—some of which could be seen more easily through a magnifying glass. The hidden message answers the riddle "What do Munchkins do when they chitchat?"

ATOM	LADYBUG
BABY	MICROCHIP
DICE	PAWN
DUST MITE	PEAS
DWARF	PEBBLE
EARPLUG	PILLS
EYE OF A NEEDLE	PORE
FLEA	PRINT
GENE	SHRIMP
GERM	SNAIL
HUMMINGBIRD	STAPLE
KITTEN	THIMBLE

```
          E R O P
        T D Y S N A I L
      M I G U B Y D A L T
      C R H E S A Y M H L
  E A G E N E T B I K E S
  D R I B G N I M M U H A
  A W S M A E B L I R A E
  L E A R P L U G I T P P
      P L R E P T M O A E
      A R F F A P M W L L
        K I T T E N B K
          N S Y B
          T E
          P O
          I F
          H A
          C N
          O E
          R E
          C D
          I L
          M E
```

86. GET THE MESSAGE?

Shaped liked a sign, the grid contains ways of getting a message across. To get the hidden message, you'll need to use a secret code. (Okay, it's not so secret.) Each letter in the message represents the letter that comes immediately before it in the alphabet. So B becomes A, C becomes B, and so forth, up to Z becomes Y. We hope you get the message, which was written by Benjamin Franklin.

BILLBOARDS

BROCHURE

CABLE

CHARADES

COURIER

E-MAIL

FAXING

LETTER

MEMO

NOTE

PHONE

POSTCARD

POSTER

SECRET CODE

SKYWRITING

SMOKE SIGNALS

STORY

TELEPATHY

TV AD

WINK

```
U  I  T  S  G  F  K  F  P  M  N  B  E
C  Z  E  L  F  N  N  F  S  H  E  T  Q
O  S  L  A  N  G  I  S  E  K  O  M  S
U  B  E  T  F  P  W  X  D  N  D  N  O
R  S  P  P  O  S  T  C  A  R  D  Y  E
I  E  A  S  T  V  A  D  R  F  F  R  M
E  U  T  J  G  B  S  U  A  X  U  O  A
R  E  H  T  L  B  K  E  H  H  P  T  I
R  B  Y  E  E  I  Y  D  C  S  F  S  L
            L  W  O
            L  R  C
            B  I  T
            O  T  E
            A  I  R
            R  N  C
            D  G  E
            S  E  S
            F  B  E
```

The flag-shaped grid contains words and phrases found in the first verse of the U.S. national anthem. The hidden message answers the riddle "What would happen if the Incredible Hulk's alter ego was covered in constellations?"

BOMBS

BRAVE

BRIGHT

BROAD

BURSTING

DAWN'S EARLY LIGHT

FREE

GALLANTLY

GLEAMING

HAILED

LAND

NIGHT

PROUDLY

RED GLARE

ROCKET'S

STARS

STILL THERE

STRIPES

TWILIGHT'S

WAVE

```
                                    S
    R  H  R  E                   B  E
    O  D  B  E  N  E  S  T     M  R  P
    C  T  H  I  D  R  H  H  G  E  O  G  O  I
    K  T  G  A  A  G  S  A  T  B  A  L  A  R
    E  H  S  T  I  L  L  T  H  E  R  E  D  T
    T  G  S  R  R  L  S  A  P  A  N  A  E  S
    S  I  B  G  A  L  E  E  R  F  E  M  V  D
    B  L  A  N  D  R  U  D  C  E  E  I  A  E
    B  Y  T  W  I  L  I  G  H  T  S  N  W
    A  L        B  U  R  S  T  I  N  G
    Y  R              N  N  E
    L  A
    D  E
    U  S
    O  N
    R  W
    P  A
    R  D
```

Shaped like a hand-held electric mixer, the grid contains utensils used in the kitchen. The hidden answer completes this line said by a carrot: "When I'm out by myself, I always think clearly…"

BOWL	PLATTER
COLANDER	POTATO MASHER
COOKIE CUTTER	POTS
FORK	SIFTER
KNIFE	SPATULA
LADLE	SPOON
PANS	TONGS
PEELER	WHISK

```
                    S  N  A  P
              B  R  E  D  N  A  L  O  C
  S  P  O  O  N        U  A  U  T  I  L
  I  E                 T  N  T  L  A  W
  F  E           B  S  T  O  P  A  L  H  O
  T  L  K  N  I  F  E  E  N  D  P  I  D  B
  E  E  E  R  K  R  O  F  L  I  S  P  G  E
  R  R  E  T  T  U  C  E  I  K  O  O  C  T
                 A  S  G  N  O  T  L
                             A
                             T
                             O
                             M
                             A
                          L  S  M
                          I  H  X
                          E  E  D
                          U  R  P
```

89. QUICKLY!

Shaped like a stopwatch, the grid contains words and phrases about being in a hurry. The hidden message answers the riddle "How do you describe a dynamite expert who's intense and in a hurry?"

DASH

"DON'T DAWDLE!"

"FAST!"

GALLOP

GO ALL OUT

HURRY

HUSTLE

MAKE HASTE

"MAKE IT SNAPPY!"

"MOVE IT!"

PUSH

RACE

RUN LIKE MAD

RUSH

SCAMPER

SCOOT

SCURRY

SKEDADDLE

TEAR

WHIP

```
      D A S H
Y         Y K           E
  R     R P E H     L
    R R E P D S G D
    O U U O A A M W A G
    H I L C N D A N M O
G W L A T S D K T E A R
T A H U S T L E S K L A
G I F I N I E H A I L C
T U E O P E H A F L O E
  O D V L K S S L N U
  B O L O A U T U U T
    S C A M P E R R
      S A S T
```

90. TAKE A PEAK

Shaped like a mountain, the grid contains things associated with mountains. The hidden message answers the riddle "What did the detective say to a crowd as he was chasing a criminal up the mountain?"

ALPS	RIDGE
ANDES	ROCKIES
ASCENT	SCENIC VIEWS
AVALANCHE	SNOWBOARDING
CLIFF	SNOWCAP
CLIMB	T-BAR
CRAGS	TRAM
GAPS	UPHILL
GLACIERS	WATERFALL
HIKE	YETI
PEAK	YODEL

```
            E
          D K O
        S A I S S
        E N H N R
      P D N O O E T
      W N W T W I O
    C R A G S B C R R
    S Y V T M O A A U
    E P A I E A L R P
  I I M L R I R G F H Y
  G K C A A R D F H I O
A S C E N T T I O A L D Y
N P O H C I L N D S L E T
M A R T H C R G A G T L I
L G S C E N I C V I E W S
```

91. MAKING A CHANGE

Shaped like a light bulb, the grid contains things you change or that are changed. The hidden message answers the riddle "Why does it take two dummies to change a light bulb on the ceiling?"

[YOUR] ATTITUDE

BOYS' VOICES

CHANNELS

[YOUR] CLOTHES

[THE] COURSE OF HISTORY

DIAPERS

[YOUR] DIET

DIRECTIONS

HAIRSTYLES

JOBS

LANES

LUCK

MENU

[YOUR] MIND

[YOUR] MOOD

PLACES

PLANS

[YOUR] ROUTINE

SEATS

[YOUR] SHOES

```
            S  E  C  A  L  P
         O  N  E  D  T  O  U  H
      D  E  N  I  T  U  O  R  C  O
   L  L  N  D  T  S  H  T  E  B  K  U
   A  C  D  I  R  E  C  T  I  O  N  S
   N  L  L  B  M  A  O  B  C  T  D  A
   E  N  D  O  O  T  U  N  H  I  T  P
   S  E  L  Y  T  S  R  I  A  H  L  A
      E  T  S  O  H  S  P  N  A  R
         O  V  U  N  E  M  N  S
            O  T  R  O  S  E
            I  S  A  F  O  L
            C  T  E  H  D  S
            E  T  S  I  H  E
            S  S  E  S  L  D
               T  B  T  O
               A  D  O  D
               E  M  R  J
               R  Y
```

92. WIN-WIN SITUATION

Shaped like a sports trophy, the grid contains things you win. The hidden message completes an often-misquoted phrase by football coach Vince Lombardi who said, "Winning isn't everything..."

APPROVAL	MEET
AWARD	MONEY
BATTLE	OSCAR
CASE	PRIZE
CONTEST	RACE
DEBATE	SPELLING BEE
DUEL	SUPER BOWL
ELECTION	TITLE
EVENT	TONY
GAME	TRIP
GRAMMY	TROPHY
LOTTERY	U.S. OPEN
MEDAL	

```
            B       U
                    T
                    T
                    D  E  E
   N  G  B     T  N  E  V  E     P  W  L
   E     A  A  N  L  B  B  S  M  R     A
   P     T  M  T  O  G  I  A  A  I     D
   O     T  S  E  T  N  O  C  T  Z     E
   S     L  N  Y  T  I  E  G  I  E     M
   U  U  E  T  M  E  L  E  C  T  I  O  N
         P  O  M  R  L  E  R  L  N
         E  A  Y  E  I  U  E
         T  R  O  P  H  Y  D
         G  B  S  N  W
               O
               T  S  W
            I  N  C  I  L
            D  R  A  W  A
         S  A  P  P  R  O  V  A  L
```

93. START AT THE END

Shaped like a dartboard with a big bull's-eye in the middle, the grid contains 20 words that each start and end with the same letter. For variety's sake, each word begins with a different letter of the alphabet. The hidden message puts three other such words together to tell you what you get if you have the smallest Eskimo canoe in a place where you wash.

ALOHA	MAXIMUM
BLOB	NEON
CATHOLIC	OLEO
DARTBOARD	PULL-UP
EARTHQUAKE	REAR
FLUFF	SPAS
GALLOPING	TICKET
HITCH	WHEW
KOOK	XEROX
LABEL	YUCKY

```
            R   T   I   N
        D   E   I   E   P   S   G   T
    E   A   R   T   H   Q   U   A   K   E
    R   R   B   A   F   F   U   L   F   B
O   T   T   I   C   K   E   T   L   L   Y   S
L   E   B   A   L           H   O   W   U   A
E   K   O   O   K           B   P   H   C   P
O   M   A   X   I   M   U   M   I   E   K   S
    T   R   L   E   U   B   T   N   W   Y
    K   D   A   O   R   C   E   G   Y   A
        C   A   T   H   O   L   I   C
            K   N   A   X
```

94. LET'S CALL IT A DAY

Shaped like the sun, the grid contains things kids often do during the course of a day. The hidden message is a parent's reminder of one more thing for you to do.

CHEW GUM	READ
DRESS	SCHOOL
EAT LUNCH	SEE FRIENDS
E-MAIL	SHOWER
HANG OUT AT MALL	SLEEP
HOMEWORK	SNACK
LAUGH	TALK
LEARN	VIDEOGAME
LEAVE HOUSE	WAKE UP
PLAY	WALK

```
                    A
      V             E                 R
         I        S N M D           E
            D D L L E A R N D A
            S E E F R I E N D S
            E K O E L L S O N T
         P  F R W G E N S K L A W
   H A N G O U T A T M A L L O
         R  H W G C V M U G W E H C E
         S  T E K L E G E A T O B
         R  M O U H S K K H P
         Y  O O U O E R T L E
         H  H C N U L T A E A
      C           P S E Y           T
   S              E                     T
                  H
```

95. IT'S A START

Shaped like a clenched hand with a finger ready to push a start button, the grid contains things you start. The hidden message answers the riddle "What did the rookie pilot say to his classmates on the first day of flight school?"

BOOK
CHORE
EATING
ENGINE
FIGHT
FIRE
FRIENDSHIP
GAME
GARDEN
HOMEWORK
JOURNEY

MOTOR
MOVING
OVER
PAYING ATTENTION
PROJECT
RACE
RIOT
RUMOR
SCHOOL
STOPWATCH
TROUBLE

```
                              R L
                            F I R E
                            K O O B
                            T E

                              S T
                            E C S
                            L H J
                          G B O E
                          F U O
                  T O     H R O L
              M F     F T C N I R
          E O     A O R F T E E E T
    E G R L R U T A Y Y D N M
  A N H O M E W O R K R D I A
  T I G O H P V N R G A S S E G
  I V R I O C T O F I G H T C A
  N O I T N E T T A G N I Y A P
  G M S T C E J O R P R P T R
```

96. ANT-ICIPATION

Each item in the word list contains the letters ANT in consecutive order. In the ant-shaped grid on the opposite page, these letters have been replaced by an 🐜. So, for example, the name SANTA CLAUS in the list will appear as S🐜ACLAUS in the grid. Now DON'T THROW A T🐜RUM and say "I C🐜DO IT!" You'll catch on in an INST🐜. The hidden message tells you about a restless animal at the zoo.

ANTARCTIC	DISTANT	PANTRY
ANTENNA	ENCHANTED	PHANTOMS
ANTHEM	GALLANTLY	PLANTS
ANTICS	GIANTS	PRAYING MANTIS
ANTIDOTES	GRANTS	RADIANT
ANTIQUE	HYDRANT	SANTA CLAUS
ANTLER	IGNORANT	SLANTS
BRILLIANT	MANTRA	TANTRUM
CANTORS	MUTANT	TARANTULA
CONSONANT	PANTING	VIBRANT

```
        D                           T
          E                   H
S        (ant)              (ant)          E  E
 L           H          E                      L
(ant)      C (ant) N                           G
 S         E N P
           A O E                    R
    L      S      (ant)
      P R A Y I N G M (ant) I S
           H S O (ant) E
  (ant) A R C T I C P H (ant) O M S
       R     G H (ant) I (ant)      U
  (ant)    I G N O R (ant) I            T
M            R           N        (ant)
A   S      D I S T (ant)    G         D
    E    T A R (ant) U L A      L
    T O (ant) R R A D I (ant)    L
    O (ant) S E C I R    L (ant)
    D (ant) I L L I R B      L
    I   N H Q A (ant) D I      L Y
   (ant) T R U M Y V V
         S P S E H              R
      (ant)                   (ant)
 S                                      P
```

Shaped like an elephant, the grid contains animals found in Africa. The hidden message is a fun fact about one of these animals.

BABOON	IMPALA
CHEETAH	LEMUR
CHIMP	LEOPARD
CIVET	LION
ELEPHANT	MONGOOSE
GAZELLE	NYALA
GIRAFFE	ORYX
GNUS	RHINOCEROS
GORILLA	SABLE
HIPPOPOTAMUS	WARTHOG
HYENA	ZEBRA

```
A  I
M
P     R  N
A     W  O  G  H     S  A  B  L  E  S  M
L     I  A  I  A  N  O  O  B  A  B  U  O  I
A  L  L  I  R  O  G  R  N  O  S  H  M  N     O
   R  N  B  A  T  I  E  L  L  E  Z  A  G     S
   E  H  F  O  H  C  C  I  V  E  T  O     L
   Z     F  L  Y  O  O  L  T  W  O  O
A     E  H  E  N  G  N  E  N  P  S
      A  N  I  A  D  M  O  O  E  A
      T  A  H  S  P  D  A  P  E  X
      E  P  R  U  M  E  L  P  A  Y
   F  E  R     N  I     A  I     R  O
   M  L  H     G  H     Y  H     O  D
   E  H  C     A  C     N  I        R
```

98. AMERICA'S FAVORITE PASTA-TIME

Shaped like a pizza pie with a slice cut out, the grid contains things in an Italian restaurant. The hidden message answers the riddle "What did the girl say to her foolish brother who had eaten too much Italian sandwich meat?"

CANNOLI	PIZZA
CLAMS	RAVIOLI
GARLIC	RICOTTA
GELATO	ROMANO
LASAGNA	SALAMI
LINGUINE	SAUSAGE
MACARONI	SPAGHETTI
MEATBALLS	TOMATO SAUCE
PASTA	VEAL
PESTO	ZITI

```
            S  H  E  M  S
   A        S  P  A  G  H  E  T  T  I
   Z  I     A  D  G  E  L  A  T  O  L  I
   T  I  S     R  I  C  O  T  T  A  I  H
I  N  T  T  K     Y  O  L  B  S  U  N  R  P
G  A  R  L  I  C     E  R  A  V  I  O  L  I
                     G  L  E  F  R  S  Z
      U  R  C  A  N  N  O  L  I  V  A  L  Z
      S  T  O  M  A  T  O  S  A  U  C  E  A
      M  L  M  S  O  F  B  S  O  A  L
      O  A  E  A  G  S  A  L  A  M  I
      P  L  I  N  G  U  I  N  E
      C  E  O  N  A
```

99. WHAT AN ICE IDEA

Shaped like an ice skate, the grid contains words and phrases associated with ice skating. The hidden message answers the riddle "What did the people say about the female ice dancer who was tight with her money?"

AXEL

BLADE

EDGE

FIGURE EIGHT

FROZEN POND

GLIDE

ICE DANCING

JUMP

LIFT

LUTZ

PAIRS

RINK

SIT SPIN

SKATE

SLIP

SPIRAL

THIN ICE

TOE LOOP

TURN

WINTER OLYMPICS

```
                  E  G  D  E
               P  T  Z  T  P  P
               I  H  A  T  M  O
               L  K  E  H  U  O
               S  Y  N  G  J  L
            T  H  I  N  I  C  E
         S  G  L  I  D  E  R  O
      A  I  D  C  S  N  E  H  T
   S  D  N  O  P  N  E  Z  O  R  F  E
W  I  A  A  L  A  R  I  P  S  U  U  T
S  T  A  X  D  B  L  A  D  E  G  F  T
C  S  H  E  E  A  I        P  I  S
P  C  L  K  R           L  F  A
I        S              T
W  I  N  T  E  R  O  L  Y  M  P  I  C  S  E
```

100. HANG IN THERE

Shaped like a trapeze artist, the grid contains things that hang, things you might hang, or words that can follow "hang." The hidden message answers the riddle "If you're performing a trapeze act, what's the worst thing you can hear from your partner?"

A LEFT	NECKLACE
BACK	NOOSE
BATS	ORNAMENT
BRANCH	PAINTING
CHANDELIER	PIÑATA
DOOR	SPIDER-MAN
EARRING	TARZAN
FIVE	TOUGH
ICICLE	YO-YO
LOOSE	YOUR HEAD

```
I                                    C
A       D                       P       N
T  T  A  R  Z  A  N  N  E  C  K  L  A  C  E
        E                           I
        H           S  T  E          N
        R           E  F  M          T
        U           T  E  O          I
        O           L                N
        Y  Y  G  E  E  A  R  R  I  N  G
            D  O  R  N  A  M  E  N  T
            O  Y  A  E  V  I  F
            O  M  T  T  L
            B  R  B  H  E
            R  E  A  L  D
            A  D  C  O  N
            N  I  K  O  A
         P  C  P     S  H  H
         I  H  S     E  C  G
         N  B           S  U
      E  A  H           A  O  N
      T  T              T  O
   G  S  O  A           F  I  N  T
```

101. CROSS-EXAMINATION

Shaped like a cross, the grid contains things you cross. The hidden message answers the question "Why didn't the boy try to solve this particular word search?"

[YOUR] ARMS
BORDER
BRIDGE
EQUATOR
[YOUR] EYES
FIELD
[YOUR] FINGERS
[YOUR] HEART
[YOUR] LEGS
LETTER T
[THE] LINE
OCEAN

ONESELF
OUT A WORD
PATHS
RIVER
ROAD
SIGNALS
SOMEONE UP
STREET
SWORDS
TIME ZONE
TOWN
WIRES

```
            I  E  Y  E  S
            E  S  F  Q  T
            N  L  L  U  N
            O  C  E  A  N
            Z  R  S  T  N
E  S  T  R  E  E  T  E  O  T  G  R  V  B  E
R  G  C  R  V  M  H  N  R  O  E  I  O  S  S
S  E  R  I  W  I  E  O  E  S  B  R  S  A  D
H  L  R  O  U  T  A  W  O  R  D  I  T  S  D
            S  R  S  I  E
            O  T  D  R  G
            M  G  R  T  N
            E  M  O  F  I
            O  W  W  I  F
            N  I  S  E  A
            E  N  I  L  R
            U  N  D  D  M
            P  A  T  H  S
```

102. START AT THE END ... AGAIN

Shaped like a teapot, the grid contains words that each begin and end with the same letter. For example, TEAPOT begins and ends with the letter T. For variety, our list contains words that begin with 20 different letters of the alphabet. (Can you think of common words for the 6 letters we didn't use: I, J, Q, U, V, and Z?) The hidden message is a sentence that contains five more words that fit this category.

ANACONDA	HURRAH	RADAR
BACKSTAB	KNOCK	RINGMASTER
BLAB	LABEL	SINGS
COMIC	MADAM	TEAPOT
DESTINED	NAPKIN	TOURNAMENT
ELSEWHERE	NICKELODEON	WHEW
FOOLPROOF	OHIO	WILLOW
GANG	OVERDO	XEROX
GOING	PLUMP	YUCKY

```
                        W   R
            F                   E   O
    E   O   O               G   H   E   M                   B   R
    L       W   O   L   L   I   W   S   A   L   I       P   L   B
    S           S   L   O   G   P   T   D   A   P       O   A
    E           G   P   P   L   N   E   A   B   K       A   T   B
    W           T   O   U   R   N   A   M   E   N   T   S   N   N
    H           D   M   I   I   O   P   G   L   O   K   I   S
    E           P   A   T   N   C   O   M   I   C   C   N
    R           Y   S   Y   G   G   T   F   A   K   H   G
    E   A       E   S   U   M   I   T   B   E   U   O   S
        A   D   N   O   C   A   N   A   L   R   V   S
                A   Y   K   S   X   O   R   E   X
                R   Y   T   D   A   R   U
                E   H   D
                O   R   O   M   M
                N   A   P   K   I   N   Y
```

103. IT'S IN THE CARDS

Shaped like a spade, the grid contains words and phrases associated with playing cards and card games. The hidden message answers this question: "If you draw a round shape on top of a full pack of playing cards, which baseball term are you suggesting?"

ACES	HEARTS
BETS	JACK
BRIDGE	KINGS
CHEAT	OLD MAID
CLUB	POKER
CRAZY EIGHTS	SHUFFLE
DEAL	SOLITAIRE
DECK	SPADE
DIAMOND	SPOONS
GIN RUMMY	SUIT
GO FISH	WIZARD

```
                I
            D   T   S
        K   I   N   G   S
      T   U   O   B   O   J   C
      S   O   R   S   A   M   R
    T   P   I   L   C   H   E   A   T
L   S   D   H   K   D   R   A   Z   I   W
A   G   I   N   R   U   M   M   Y   E   D
E   O   O   P   S   T   R   A   E   H   N
D   F   S   O   L   I   T   A   I   R   E
D   I   B   K   C   E   D   B   G   D   E
    S   C   E   L   F   F   U   H   S
    H   K   R   T       C   L   T   I
        R   C       S       C   S
                    E
                L   C   E
            S   P   A   D   E
```

213

104. TRAINING SESSION

Shaped like a caboose sitting on a railroad track, the grid contains things associated with trains. The hidden message answers the riddle "What did the girl say to the boy who could think only about trains?"

ACELA

"ALL ABOARD!"

AMTRAK

BAGGAGE

BERTH

BOX CAR

BULLET TRAIN

CABOOSE

CONDUCTOR

COUPLER

DIESEL

ORIENT EXPRESS

PASSENGERS

PLATFORM

RAIL

SPUR

STATION

SWITCH

TRIP

WHISTLE

```
            H   T   R   E   B
                C   E   S
                L   T   R
S   S   E   R   P   X   E   T   N   E   I   R   O   H   E
    G   D   I   E   S   E   L   S   A   W   I
    A   D   Y   I   P   P   I   R   T   O   S
    G   U   H   V   U   E   A   C   E   L   A
    G   W   G   O   R   O   T   M   S   A   O
L   A   N   C   O   N   D   U   C   T   O   R       E
I   B   T   A   L   L   A   B   O   A   R   D       R
R   A   C   X   O   B   U   L   L   E   T   T   R   A   I   N   A
R   C           O                   I           K   K
        M   O   I           N   O   D
        S                   N
S   R   E   G   N   E   S   S   A   P   L   A   T   F   O   R   M
```

105. LOOKING FOR FOSSILS

Shaped like a dinosaur's head, the grid contains words associated with dinosaurs. The hidden message answers the riddle "What do you say to a T. Rex who throws tantrums when he doesn't win?"

ALLOSAURUS

BONE

CHOMP

CLAWS

EGGS

EXTINCT

FOSSILS

JAWS

JURASSIC

PALEONTOLOGIST

PLANT EATER

RAPTORS

REPTILES

ROAM

SKULL

SLASH

TAIL

TAR PITS

TEETH

T. REX

```
              H S A L S
            O W C H O M P
        B H J U R A S S I C D L
      O M A O R N L A S T   B A
      E X T I N C T E P W     A N
  A     D   I   E   N   T A I L T
                          O J L E
      O   X   S   F       O S R O A
  R P A L E O N T O L O G I S T
  E S T I P R A T E S L G S A E
  O S R E P T I L E S E K U R
                    T I U R
                    H L U E
                    L S R
```

106. QUEUING UP

Shaped like a letter Q, the grid contains words and phrases that each contain a Q. The hidden message is a sensible sentence that contains four more Q words.

AQUA

CIRQUE DU SOLEIL

CROQUET

DISQUALIFY

EARTHQUAKE

EQUIPS

MOSQUITO

PLAQUE

QANTAS

Q-TIP

QUARTERS

QUEASY

QUEENS

QUIET

QUILTED

QUINCE

QUINTUPLET

QUIZ

QUOTATION

SEQUEL

SQUALL

SQUIGGLY

SQUINT

SQUIRRELS

SQUIRT GUN

```
          Q A O S S Q
        C U U T Y E I P D S
      Q I D I S Q U A L I F Y
    U N R U A U Y L G G I U Q S
      C E Q E E         E Z E Q L
  E R S U L             E K S E D
  I O Q E               A R R N
  M Q U D               U E R T
  D U I U       O N A   Q T I P
  S E R S         Q O Z   H R U S
  S T T O S         Q I U T A Q A
    Q G L R A         U T R U S
    E U E I Q T E I U Q E A Q A
      N I Q U I N T U P L E T
        L N A Q Q A U L A R N O
          T P L A Q U E   I S U
                        U M Q
```

107. MELLOW YELLOW

Shaped like a sunflower, the grid contains things that are always or often yellow. The hidden message names three characters who are predominantly yellow.

BANANA	PENCIL
BUTTER	POST-IT
CANARY	RAIN SLICKER
CORN	SCHOOL BUS
DAFFODIL	SMILEY FACE
DANDELION	TAXI
LEMON	TENNIS BALL
MANGO [INSIDES]	WHEAT
PEEPS	YOLK

```
                B       I
        W       C       O       G               B
I               H       A   R   G   Y           D
    A           E   N   N   N   P   O   T               R
    N   D   L   A   T   A   E   E   L           E
B   U   T   T   E   R   T   M   N   W   E   K
    E   T   M   Y   Y   N   C   A   C   O   R   N
D   A   F   F   O   D   I   L   I   I   B   A
    T   N   N   S   U   B   L   O   O   H   C   S
    D       A   B   P   O   S   T   I   T
        A   X   P   N   M   P   I           K
    L           I   O   I   A   E               C
L           A       I   L           E
        R           L   E               P
                    E   Y
                    D   F
                    N   A
                    A   C
                    D   E
                    H   U
```

108. PLAYING IN THE PARK

Shaped like a squirrel, the grid contains things found in a park. The hidden message answers this question: "If birds are crazy about bird seed, what can you say about squirrels?"

BALL	KITES
BENCH	LAMPPOST
BIKES	PATHS
BIRD	PICNIC TABLES
BUSHES	SOCCER
CONCERT	SQUIRREL
DOGS	STATUE
FRISBEE	SWING
GRASS	TENNIS COURT
JOGGERS	TREES
KIDS	WALKER

```
                S       B
                S   D   I   K
            R   E   A   T   R   H
            E   L   B   R   E   D
            K   B   U       G   Y
        R   L   A   S
        P   A   T   H   S               E
    S   N   U   C   W   C   E   T   T   S
  F   Q   O   H   A   B   O   I   S   A
T   R   U   O   C   S   I   N   N   E   T
R   I   I       N   C   K   B   C   C   U   O
E   S   R       E   B   E   K   I   T   E   S   U
E   B   R       B   A   S   R   P   D   T   R   N
S   E   E       L   A   M   P   P   O   S   T
    E   L       L   U   S   W   I   N   G
        T       J   O   G   G   E   R   S   S
```

223

109. TUTTI-FRUITY

Shaped like an apple, the grid contains various kinds of fruit. The hidden message is a trivia fact about how strawberry seeds are different from the seeds of most other fruits.

APPLE	LIME
APRICOT	NECTARINE
BANANA	ORANGE
BERRY	PAPAYA
CANTALOUPE	PEACH
CHERRY	PEAR
DATE	PLUM
GRAPE	PRUNE
KIWI	TANGERINE
KUMQUAT	WATERMELON

```
                    T
                 H
              N
              O
     E  Y  A  R  L  R  E  P  N
  Y  G  R  A  P  E  E  E  R  O  B
  R  T  N  I  K  M  A  N  U  A  E
  R  G  E  N  I  R  E  G  N  A  T
  E  S  C  L  W  E  I  A  E  D  A
  H  H  T  E  I  T  N  B  K  U  D
  C  C  A  N  T  A  L  O  U  P  E
  T  A  R  P  O  W  O  B  M  N  T
     E  I  A  C  H  E  E  Q  M
     P  N  P  I  R  L  E  U  O
        E  A  R  P  U  L  A
        T  Y  P  S  P  I  T
        A  A     D  E
```

110. DESK JOCKEY

Shaped like a Scotch tape dispenser, the grid contains things found on or near a desk at home. The hidden message answers the riddle "What do you get when you combine a thing used to surround a bunch of papers with a thing used to cover a cut?"

COMPUTER	PAPER
DESK	PENCILS
ENVELOPES	PENS
FILE CABINET	PHONE
FOLDER	POST-ITS
HOLE PUNCH	RULER
LAMP	SCISSORS
MARKER	SCOTCH TAPE
MODEM	STAMPS
OUTLET	STAPLES

```
      Y K M O M S
    U G O S A N E H
  C T D T R E D L O F
S O E A K P A D R L U
C M M E       B O E B
I P R         U P
S U E         T U           R S
S T L         L N           L B
O E A A     N E C D       I A R
R R M P I E P A T H C T O C S U
S E P O L E V N E P H O N E L
  D F I L E C A B I N E T E
    S T I T S O P A P E R
```

227

111. HATS ENTERTAINMENT

Every item in the word list contains the letters HAT in consecutive order. When these letters appear in the hat-shaped grid, each HAT has been replaced by a 🎩. So, for example, the phrase ALL THAT JAZZ would appear in the grid as ALLT🎩JAZZ. We hope t🎩's somewhat helpful. The hidden message is an angry exchange of words between a scolding parent and a defiant child.

BOOBY HATCH

CAPE HATTERAS

CHATTANOOGA

CHATTERBOX

EMPHATIC

HARD HAT

HATBOX

HATCHBACK

HATCHET

HATLESS

HAT PIN

HAT TRICK

"I HATE YOU!"

[THE] MAD HATTER

MANHATTAN

SHATTER

"SO WHAT?"

"THATAWAY!"

THATCHED

TOP HAT

WHAT IF…

"WHAT'S UP, DOC?"

T 🎩 S S E L 🎩 🎩
C 🎩 T A N O O G A D
E R R R S E M N E O
M E I E U A F H G H
P T C T N O C I W S
🎩 🎩 K 🎩 F 🎩 Y T 🎩 O
I D T E T A N T S W
C A R P W E E I U 🎩
T 🎩 N M T A 🎩 R R S P W 🎩 🎩
B O O B Y 🎩 C H E T B D 🎩 Y B O
U P T T H I I 🎩 E Y O U O N
🎩 C H B A C K K C X

112. CAPITOL LETTERS

Shaped like the top of the U.S. Capitol building, the grid contains words and phrases associated with Washington, D.C. The hidden message lists some unusual animals that were presidential pets.

BILLS

CABINET

[SUPREME] COURT

[THE CAPITOL] DOME

LAWS

LINCOLN MEMORIAL

[THE] MALL

PENTAGON

POLITICS

POTOMAC [RIVER]

PRESIDENT

REFLECTING POOL

SENATE

TREASURY

[THE] WEST WING

[THE] WHITE HOUSE

```
                S
                E
              L N M
              Y A A
            C R T W A
          W E U E S S A
          P R E S I D E N T
          O R T A U A O C C
        O L W O E T O N M P A
        N I D E R V B H O E L
        N T E U T I N T E L A
    D G A I O I L N O G A T N E P
    L I N C O L N M E M O R I A L
    R Y C S S C A B I N E T O H W
    R E F L E C T I N G P O O L W
```

113. CAT-22

Shaped like the head of a cat (or is it a mouse?) with whiskers and ears, the grid contains 22 items associated with cats. The hidden message is a punny question.

CALICO

DECLAW

FINICKY EATERS

HAIR BALL

HISS

KITTENS

LEAP

LIE IN THE SUN

LITTER BOX

MANX

MEOW

MOUSER

PAWS

POUNCE

PURR

SCRATCH

SIAMESE

SLEEP

STRETCH

TAIL

WHISKERS

YAWN

```
    S  I  E                          F  C  L
    A  R  S  S                    T  A  I  L
       C  E  A  T  T  M  P  F  L  E  B
       M  K  U  R  E  A  I  I  L
       A  R  S  E  E  C  N  N  L
       I  S  L  I  O  T  I  X  A
       S  S  D  I  H  I  C  T  B
    W  O  E  M  S  E  T  W  K  H  R  B  U
 T        T  O  S  C  C  T  Y  L  I        I
       S  S  U  C  N  T  L  E  Y  A  S
    H     N  S  R  U  A  A  A  R  H     S
       W  E  A  O  P  W  T  W  B
       A  T  R  T  P  N  A  E  R  C  O
    P        A  C  T  T  A  R  S        X
          T  H  R  I  U  S  O
          P  H  P  K  E
```

Shaped like the head of a man with a very big nose, the grid contains things that run. The hidden message answers the riddle "Why is this man's body confused?"

CARS

CHEETAH

COMPUTER PROGRAM

DEER

DISHWASHER

DOGS

DYES

FAUCET

FURNACE

HORSE

JOGGER

MASCARA

MOTOR

MOWER

NEWSPAPER STORY

NOSE

PAINT

[A] PLAY

POLITICIAN

RACER

RIVER

SCARED PERSON

STOCKINGS

[A] WATCH

```
            C D Y E S H
          P A I N T I M S
          N R S T N A O S P
          E S H E S N G G O
        S W S W C E O R N L
    R R U S ● A U D S O I I
  N N O S E P R S A S R T K T
A C H E E T A H H F N E O C I
M A R G O R P R E T U P M O C
        D E H R I D D R T I
        R G R I V E R S A
        S S F G E W R E R N
      W A T C H O P A A R
    E T S O M M L J C E
    L F U R N A C E S
          Y Y L R
```

115. POLICE SEARCH

Shaped like a policeman's badge, the grid contains words and phrases associated with police work. The hidden message answers the riddle "What did the cop's wife tell her kids to do to be polite?"

ARREST

BADGE

BEAT

CHASE

COFFEE

COPS

CRIME

DETECTIVE

DONUTS

DRAGNET

FRISK

GUNS

HANDCUFFS

LAW AND ORDER

NIGHTSTICK

PATROL

PRECINCT

RAID

RAP SHEET

SEARCH WARRANT

SQUAD CAR

SUSPECT

SWEEP

UNDERCOVER

```
            C  H  A  S  E
   L  R  A  S  U  S  P  E  C  T  A  E  B
   L  A  W  R  A  C  D  A  U  Q  S  V  A
      P  W  H  P  A  T  R  O  L  Y  I
      S  S  A  P  R  E  C  I  N  C  T
      H  K  N  N  S  S  H  A  Y  S  C
      E  S  D  U  D  S  W  E  E  P  E
   P  E  I  C  O  G  O  A  R  L  I  T  C
   C  T  R  U  N  D  E  R  C  O  V  E  R
   C  O  F  F  E  E  A  R  D  C  E  D  I
   R  A  P  F  E  G  D  A  B  E  N  D  M
   T  A  H  S  A  T  E  N  G  A  R  D  E
      N  I  G  H  T  S  T  I  C  K  N
         D  O  N  U  T  S  K
            Y  O  U
```

116. CHOCK FULL OF CHOCOLATE

Shaped like a chocolate kiss, the grid contains things that are always or often made with chocolate. The hidden message completes this bit of humorous advice: "Eating chocolate gives you the energy…"

BONBON

BROWNIES

DEVIL'S FOOD CAKE

ECLAIR

FUDGE

FUDGSICLE

HOT COCOA

KISS

KIT KAT [BAR]

MALTED

MILK SHAKE

MINTS

MOUSSE

MUD PIE

OREO

PARFAIT

PUDDING

SNICKERS [BAR]

SUNDAE

TOOTSIE ROLL

TRUFFLE

TURTLE

```
        T  E
     O     S     E  A  T
           S              A
           E  U           W
           I     O        H
           E  N  R     M
        O  G  W  I  P
        N  D  O  A  E
     I  T  U  R  L  A  L
  D  A  H  F  B  C  D  E  L
  D  K  O  A  O  T  E  N  T  M  O
U  T  R  I  N  U  T  R  U  F  F  L  E
P  I  E  T  B  R  C  H  C  S  T  N  I  M  M
K  T  O  O  T  S  I  E  R  O  L  L  O  C  A
I  O  N  L  F  U  D  G  S  I  C  L  E  L  L
S  R  E  K  C  I  N  S  O  R  E  O  A  T  T
S  E  I  P  D  U  M  I  L  K  S  H  A  K  E
E  E  K  A  C  D  O  O  F  S  L  I  V  E  D
```

117. WHAT'S YOUR NUMBER?

Shaped like a triangle, the grid contains words that have a numerical prefix. For example, TRI- means "three," and a TRIPLE is a three-base hit. Similarly, DEC- means "ten," and a DECADE is a period of ten years. (The meanings of the prefixes are given on page 351.) The hidden message is a sports-related sentence that contains two more words with numerical prefixes.

BICEPS

BINOCULARS

BIPED

CENTIPEDES

CENTURY

DECADE

DECIMAL

OCTOPI

PENTAGON

QUARTET

QUINTUPLETS

TRIPLE

TRIPOD

UNICYCLE

```
                    E
                 T  D  H
                 E  A  Y
              T  T  C  R  R
              S  I  E  U  A
           T  H  E  D  T  L  E
           T  E  T  D  N  R  R
        L  A  M  I  C  E  D  A  I
        E  D  I  E  S  C  P  A  U
     S  T  E  L  P  U  T  N  I  U  Q
     B  I  P  E  D  O  P  I  R  T  D
  E  C  I  C  P  E  N  T  A  G  O  N  A
  T  R  I  H  L  U  N  I  C  Y  C  L  E
O  T  B  N  S  R  A  L  U  C  O  N  I  B  C
```

118. PLAYTIME

Shaped like a piano, the grid contains things people play. The hidden message answers the riddle "What did the music-loving baseball player like to play?"

BINGO	PINBALL
BY THE RULES	POOL
CATCH	POSSUM
CHESS	RISK
DOMINOES	ROLE
DUMB	TO WIN
FAIR	VIDEO GAME
GOLF	VIOLIN
HOUSE	WITH FIRE
MAKE-BELIEVE	YAHTZEE

```
          P  S  E  W
          I  H  E  I
          N  O  Z  T  S  R  F  A  I  R
       T  B  Y  T  H  E  R  U  L  E  S  S  T
    O  A  P  H  F  L  V  V  T  O  W  I  N  A
    L  N  A  I  O  S  I  B  D  G  H  P
 C  L  P  Y  R  R  S  O  D  O  M  I  N  O  E  S
 M  A  K  E  B  E  L  I  E  V  E  U  K  S  I  R
    T  I  H  I  L  O  O  P           D  S  A
    C  N  B  I  N  G  O              U
       H  N     A                    M
       O        M
                E
```

119. THE RULING CLASS

Shaped like a five-pointed crown, the grid contains words associated with kings, kingdoms, and royalty. The hidden message mentions two kings that are a part of your everyday life.

CASTLE

COLONIES

CROWN

CZAR

DUKES

EARLS

KING

MAJESTY

PALACE

PRINCE

REALM

REGAL

REIGN

ROYAL WEDDING

RULER

SCEPTRE

THRONES

TIARA

WARS

"YES, SIRE"

```
              E
            T C H
    C       K N T             Y
      O I   N N I C K     I E
      N L G W A R N A A S S
      N O R D P E G S E
  B   R A N A S L I K T
    I C   N L I C R U G     L E
    R O Y A L W E D D I N G E
      K C I W A P S L R A E
      E Z N L A T R E L U R
        A M T H R O N E S
        R M A J E S T Y G
```

120. CATCHING COLD

Shaped like a snowflake, the grid contains things that are always or often cold. The hidden message is a Tom Swifty, a type of wordplay in which the adverb creates a pun.

ANTARCTICA	IGLOO
CASE	OCEAN
DEEP SPACE	RINK
DOG'S NOSE	SNOW
EVEREST	SWEAT
FRONT	TRAIL
FROST	WIND
ICE AGE	WINTER

```
                I
             H  N  E
    W  R     A  A  V        E  L
       I  I  T  F  E  E  W     C  I
    W  A  N  T  A  R  C  T  I  C  A  S  E
       K  D  E  O  O  E  N  R  P
       I  N  S  O  N  T  G  T  E  S  R
       T  L  N  T  S  A  E  A  P
    D  O  G  S  N  O  S  E  R  A  E  I  D
       I  T     O  O  W  C  M     E  W
    C     O     R  L  I     D     S
             D     F     L
                   Y
```

121. HAIRPIECES

Shaped like a head of hair, the grid contains things associated with hair. The hidden message answers this riddle about a sharpshooting cowgirl: "How is her favorite hairstyle like her enjoyment of gunfire?"

BAD HAIR DAY	CURLER
BARBER SHOP	DREADLOCKS
BLEACHED BLONDE	FLIP
BOBBY PINS	PIGTAIL
BRUNETTE	PONYTAIL
BRUSH	RINSE
COLOR	SALON
COMB	SHAMPOO
CONDITIONER	SNARL
CONK	STYLE
CORNROWS	TINTS
COWLICK	WASH

```
            W  A  S  H  S
         B  K  C  I  L  W  O  C  H
         C  O  N  D  I  T  I  O  N  E  R
      E  B  B  B  A  D  H  A  I  R  D  A  Y
      E  R  B  T  L           S  T  N  I  T
   F  D  U  Y  I              K  B  R  P  S
   L  N  N  P                 R  E  O  K
   I  O  E  I                 U  L  H  C
   P  L  T  N                 S  R  S  O
   I  B  T  S                 H  U  R  L
   G  D  E  N                 A  C  E  D
   T  E  S  A                 M  E  B  A
   A  H  N  R  S           N  P  M  R  E
   I  C  I  L  S           C  O  B  A  R
   L  A  R  T  A           C  O  L  B  D
      E  Y  N              O  L  A
   G  L  S                 N  O  S
   E  B                    K  R
```

122. TO TOP IT ALL OFF

Shaped like a blouse, the grid contains things you wear at or above the waist. The hidden message completes the joke "When a shirt and a skirt play games, the skirt loses every time because…"

BELT

BERET

BIBS

BLOUSE

BONNET

BOW TIE

BULLETPROOF VEST

DASHIKI

EARMUFFS

GOGGLES

HAIR NETS

HELMET

HOOD

JERSEY

KERCHIEF

NECKLACE

PULLOVER

SASH

SHIRT

SKI MASK

TANK TOP

TIARA

VEIL

V-NECK

```
    A H S V           T T H L
  B O N N E T       I S E I R B
  O F E I H C R E K E E M A E
D T C     B O W T I E V A   L R L
W K       E A R M U F F S     E A
A Y       S T A N K T O P     T H
          I S E L G G O G
          K E E H N D R Y
          I C S T S U P E
          H A I R N E T S
          S L B I B S E R
          A K P H O U L E
          D C N S T O L J
          R E V O L L U P
          O N T L E B B P
```

Shaped like arrows going in different directions, the grid contains things you ask for, like DIRECTIONS or HELP. The hidden message answers the question "What did the jet pilot ask for while flying in a pattern with other jets?"

ADVICE	[THE] MOON
ALMS	MORE
A LOT	[A PHONE] NUMBER
[A] DATE	[YOUR] PATIENCE
DIRECTIONS	PERMISSION
[A] FAVOR	[A] RAISE
FOOD	[A] SECOND CHANCE
HELP	SILENCE
"…IT BY NAME!"	[THE] TIME
MERCY	TROUBLE

```
                  S
               I  E  N
            E  F  C  T  P
         M  O  C  O  I  E  R
            E  E  N  M  R
      F     C  R  D  E  M     M
   O  D  I  R  E  C  T  I  O  N  S
   O  T  V  A  R  M  H  Y  S  T  R  F  S
D  T  D  R  O  O  A  A  I  S  A  A  A  I  O  N
   A  I  M  O  N  N  N  N  I  V  L  P  F
   T  N  O  U  Y  C  S  O  E  M  R
      E     M  B  E  R  N     S
            B  T  L  C  H
         M  E  I  E  E  A  T
            R  A  L  O  T
            P  I  O
               N
```

253

124. NAME-DROPPING

Shaped like a check mark, the grid contains words that begin or end with a common first name, like SAM as in SAMe or MARK as in check MARK. The names may be boys' or girls' names and will be three- or four-letters in length. After you're done, go back to the word list and see if you can find every name. (To check your answers, see the name list on page 351.) The hidden message names two countries that end with boys' names.

ANNOYED	JANITOR	THINGAMABOB
BENT	KITE	TIMID
BRICK	LOUD	TISSUE
CANDY	MASTODON	TOMORROW
CREATED	PATTER	VICE
GENETICS	SPOKEN	WEST
IRON	STUDY	

```
                    T  I  M  I  D
                 P  G  A  A  E
                 B  E  N  T  K
              Y  D  N  A  C
              I  O  E  E  T
           S  Y  R  T  H
           E  C  I  I  T
        D  A  K  N  C
N  D  P  I        T  J  G  E  S
N  Y  R  A  M  I  O  A  E  K
N  O  D  O  T  S  A  M  N  C  A
N  E  D  U  S  T  A  O  I  I
   R  K  U  T  B  E  R  T  V
   E  O  O  S  B  R  O
      B  P  L  K  O  R
      T  S  E  W
```

Shaped like a unicycle, the grid contains things with wheels. The hidden message answers the riddle "What do you get when you combine a road-smoothing vehicle with a pair of in-line skates?"

CABOOSE	SEMI
CHARIOT	SKATEBOARD
COUPE	SUVS
DUNE BUGGY	TANK
GO-KART	TAXI
HOT ROD	TRACTOR
JITNEY	WAGON
MOPED	

```
                S
        S   E   M   I
                O
                P
                E
                D
                R
                A
                O
        R   S   B   T
    E   U   O   E   A   T
  C   V   H   O   T   R   O   D
E   S   O   O   B   A   C   M   R   I
W   O   L   U   K   K   N   A   T   X
L   A   E   O   P   S   R   B   R   A
Y   G   G   U   B   E   N   U   D   T
    L   T   O   I   R   A   H   C
    Y   E   N   T   I   J
        A   D   E   S
```

257

126. FILL IN THE WORDS

Shaped like a pail, the grid contains things you fill or fill up. The hidden message is the name of everyone's favorite gas station attendant.

AUDITORIUM

BALLOON

BATHTUB

BIRD FEEDER

BOWL

CAR TRUNK

DUMP TRUCK

FISH TANK

GAS TANK

GLASS

GROCERY CART

HAMPER

HOLE

PAIL

PIGGY BANK

POOL

SINK

SQUIRT GUN

TEETH

TIRE

TRASH CAN

VASE

WASHER

WATER BOTTLE

```
              L  I  A  P  T  T
           O                    I
        O                          R
     P                                E
     I                                L
     G                                T
     G  G  R  O  C  E  R  Y  C  A  R  T
     Y  G  A  S  T  A  N  K  H  M  A  O
     B  T  W  Q  B  A  T  H  T  U  B  B
     A  K  N  U  R  T  R  A  C  I  I  R
     N  O  U  I  H  A  M  P  E  R  N  E
     K  C  U  R  T  P  M  U  D  O  S  T
     K  N  A  T  H  S  I  F  O  T  S  A
     H  B  L  G  E  D  E  L  B  I  A  W
     E  O  P  U  H  E  L  E  N  D  L  I
     L  W  L  N  D  A  T  K  S  U  G  R
     R  L  U  E  B  R  E  H  S  A  W  P
        T  R  A  S  H  C  A  N  P  V
```

127. COLOR I.D.

Shaped like a paintbrush, the grid contains the names of various colors. The hidden message answers the riddle "How should a zombie movie never be filmed?"

APRICOT	LIME GREEN
BEIGE	MILK-WHITE
BLACK	NAVY BLUE
BRICK RED	OLIVE
BRONZE	ORANGE
EBONY	PINK
GOLD	SCARLET
GRAY	SILVER
HAZEL	TEAL
INDIGO	VIOLET
IVORY	YELLOW

```
            I
         N  L  E
         E     B
         U  D  O
         L  E  N
         B  R  Y
         Y  K  E
         V  C  L
         A  I  L
         N  R  O
      L  D  I  B  W  L  V
   E  I  O  B  D  I  N  E  S
T  G  M  I  L  K  W  H  I  T  E
O  N  E  O  A  I  I  L  G  E  G
C  A  G  C  C  P  V  V  L  A  I
I  R  R  G  K  E  I  E  O  L  E
R  O  E  O  R  E  Z  N  O  R  B
P  T  E  L  R  A  C  S  K  L  Y
A     N     H     Y     O     R
```

Shaped like a jack-o'-lantern, the grid contains words and phrases associated with Halloween. The hidden message answers the riddle "Why are the goofy neighbors putting little hot dogs in kids' trick-or-treat bags?"

BLACK CATS	MASK
COSTUME	NIGHT
DEMONS	OCTOBER
DEVIL	PRANK
GHOST	SCARY
GHOUL	SKELETON
HAUNTED HOUSE	"TRICK OR TREAT!"
HORROR MOVIE	UNDEAD
HOWL	VAMPIRE
JACK-O'-LANTERN	WITCH

```
        T   H

                S

                N

        G   H   O   S   T

    E   H   V   A   M   P   I   R   E

      Y   O   R   S   K   E   L   E   T   O   N

  E   U   G   I   ▲   L   D   V   ▲   I   N   R   R

  L   C   G       ▲       W       ▲       O   E   E

  H   O   R   R   O   R   M   O   V   I   E   T   B

  C   S   C   A   R   Y   ▲   T   H   G   I   N   O

  T   T   R   I   C   K   O   R   T   R   E   A   T

  I   U   N   D   E   A   D   D   E   V   I   L   C

  W   M           U       T           O   O

  H   E                               K   A

  L   L   O   W                   E   E   C   M

  N   E   S   U   O   H   D   E   T   N   U   A   H

      I   B   L   A   C   K   C   A   T   S   J

          E   S   P   R   A   N   K
```

129. READ ALL ABOUT IT

Shaped like a mail box, the grid contains things you read. The hidden message lists three more things you might read.

ARTICLE	MAGAZINE
BIBLE	MAPS
COMIC BOOK	MENU
E-MAIL	NEWSPAPER
EYE CHART	POEM
FINE PRINT	SIGN
INSTRUCTIONS	SKYWRITING
LETTER	STORY

```
        F L I
        I   P S
        N
        E
    M R E P A P S W E N A
    M L M M R U I S G I R C
    R A E A I G T H N T S E
  R I N P T N E L B I B T E
  L U I N S T R U C T I O N
M A G A Z I N E L O I P R O
T R A H C E Y E R M R E Y T
            I W
            C Y
            B K
            O S
            O E
            K R
```

130. SLICE OF LIFE

Shaped like a slice of bread, the grid contains sandwich ingredients and types of sandwiches. The hidden message answers the question "What did the kid say when he was asked, 'What's your favorite and least favorite sandwich meat?'"

AVOCADO	ONION
BOLOGNA	PASTRAMI ON RYE
BREAD	PEANUT BUTTER
CHEESE	SALAMI
CHICKEN	SHRIMP SALAD
EGG SALAD	SPAM
FALAFEL	SPICED HAM
FISH	TOMATO
JELLY	TUNA MELT
LETTUCE	TURKEY
MAYO	WHOLE WHEAT
MEAT LOAF	WRAP
MUSTARD	

```
      I   M   A   L   A   S   H   C   S
    T   U   R   K   E   Y   P   H   A   H   W
  P   A   S   T   R   A   M   I   O   N   R   Y   E
  M   E   S   E   E   H   C   C   J   A   I   T   I
  S   H   A   B   G   K   E   E   P   S   M   U   T
  W   V   N   E   G   L   D   A   N   P   N
  E   O   N   U   L   S   H   D   T   S   A
  L   C   M   Y   T   S   A   O   Y   A   M
  O   A   E   A   I   B   M   L   T   L   E
  H   D   A   F   P   A   U   E   A   A   L
  W   O   T   H   T   S   E   T   L   D   T
  B   O   L   O   G   N   A   T   T   A   I
  V   N   O   I   N   O   E   U   R   E   W
  D   R   A   T   S   U   M   C   U   R   R
  R   S   F   A   L   A   F   E   L   B   T
```

131. SHELL GAME

Shaped like a shell, the grid contains words and phrases spelled with double L's, like SHELL. In fact, 10 of the items have two sets of double L's, like VOLLEYBALL. The hidden message is the name of a legendary person who has double L's in both his first and his last name.

ALL'S WELL	GOLLY	QUILL
BALLET	HELLO	REALLY
BELL	HILLBILLY	ROLL CALL
BILLION	ILL WILL	SHELL
CELL	ILLEGALLY	SKILLFULLY
COLLIE	JELLY ROLL	TOLL CALL
DILLY-DALLY	MALL	VILLAGE
DOLL	MILL	VOLLEYBALL
FELL	PILLOW	WALLET
FILLY	POLLIWOG	

```
          W  V  L  T  J
       L  H  I  L  L  E  F  P  T
    L  L  L  I  W  L  L  I  I  O  T
 I  L  L  U  C  L  L  L  O  L  L  E  H
M  I  A  Q  E  Y  L  L  A  D  Y  L  L  I  D
I  G  C  L  R  H  O  A  B  L  L  C  L  Y  O
E  L  L  O  I  W  S  M  Y  I  O  A  A  A  L
M  N  L  A  L  L  S  W  E  L  L  L  W  T  L
    L  O  E  S  K  I  L  L  F  U  L  L  Y
       R  I  G  O  W  I  L  L  O  P  Y
          E  L  A  E  G  O  L  L  Y
             A  L  L  E  V  L  L
                L  I  L  E  L
                   L  B  Y
                      Y
```

132. PACKING A PUNCH

Shaped like a boxing glove, the grid contains words and phrases associated with boxing. The hidden message answers the riddle "Why is the end of a boxing match like a gorgeous person?"

BOUT

BOXER

CORNER

FIGHT

GLASS JAW

GLOVES

HEAVYWEIGHT

JABS

JUDGES

LOW BLOW

MAIN EVENT

MOUTHGUARD

PUNCH

REFEREE

RING

ROBE

ROUNDS

SAVED BY THE BELL

SPAR

TITLE

TOWEL

UPPERCUT

```
        R  O  U  N  D  S
     H  E  O  B  P  E  A  C
     E  N  A  B  U  P  V  S        S  S
     A  R  E  F  E  R  E  E        E  F
     V  O  P  E  E  V  D  R  A  G  I
     Y  C  T  U  O  B  B  A  C  D  G
     W  M  C  L  N  H  Y  P  O  U  H
     E  O  G  F  T  C  T  S  H  J  T
     I  U  L  E  T  M  H  I  S  N  A
     G  T  A  B  O  X  E  R  E  T
     H  H  S  K  W  N  B  V  I
     T  G  S  O  E  O  E  T
     C  U  J  R  L  N  L  K
        A  A  A  I  E  L
        R  W  A  B  N  O
        D  M  U  T  S  G
```

133. FIELD DAY

Shaped like a scarecrow, the grid contains words associated with growing crops. The hidden message answers the riddle "What did the farmer say he could grow even if weather conditions kept getting worse?"

ACRES	HAYSTACK
BUSHEL	HOES
CORN	OATS
COTTON BALES	PLOW
CROWS	REAPER
FARMER	SEED
FIELD	SOIL
GROW	STALKS
HARVEST	TRACTOR

```
            I  C  A
            N  G  R  O  W
            A     O     L
            T
            W  C  A
C  O  T  T  O  N  B  A  L  E  S  W  O  R  C
            Y  B  N  R  O  C  A
            D  U  T  S  C
            G  L  S  R  R
            O  E  H
            W  S  V  I  E
         R  E  M  R  A  F  L
         E  S  T  A  L  K  S
         P  O     H     I  W
         A  D     A     L  O
      S  E        Y        L  S
      E  R        S        P  T
   S  O           T        A  D
   E  H           A        O  R
                  C
                  K
```

134. WHAT'S THE QUESTION?

Shaped like a question mark, the grid contains 18 common questions. The hidden message gives a different answer to the famous question "Why did the chicken cross the road?"

AGAIN?

ARE WE THERE YET?

ARE YOU SURE?

CAN I?

HAD ENOUGH?

HUNGRY?

HUNH?

MAY I?

OH YEAH?

READY?

REALLY?

WHAT'S NEXT?

WHAT'S UP?

WHEN?

WHICH ONE?

WHO IS IT?

WHO'S THERE?

WHO WON?

```
        T W H A T S U P
      O S H A D E N O U G H
  Y D A E R U S U O Y E R A
  T E Y E R E H T E W E R A
  W H E N           H H O W W
  O O W             O H H A
                    I O G W
                  C S A H
            H H T I A
            E O H N T
          W N E U S
          E R R N
          E A E G
          S X A R
          T N L Y
          T C L H
          M A Y I

            I C
          C K A E
          H U N H
            N I
```

135. KNOCK KNOCK

Every item in the word list contains the letters DOOR in consecutive order. When these letters appear in the door-shaped grid, each DOOR has been replaced by a 🚪. So, for example, the word BACKDOOR would appear in the grid as BACK 🚪. The hidden message answers the riddle "What did the boy say to the cute girl NEXT 🚪?"

BARNDOOR

CAR DOOR

CLOSE THE DOOR

DOORBELL

DOORFRAME

DOOR HANDLE

DOORKNOB

DOORMAN

DOORMAT

DOOR PRIZE

DOORWAY

FOLDING DOOR

FRONT DOOR

GARAGE DOOR

GO DOOR TO DOOR

"IT'S DO OR DIE!"

KNOCK AT THE DOOR

OUTDOORSMAN

REFRIGERATOR DOOR

REVOLVING DOOR

SCREEN DOOR

SLIDING DOORS

STAY INDOORS

TRAPDOOR

```
O I S T A Y I N □ S T
U H A I E L D N A H □
T M           M N
□ G           K □
S O           K R
M □           N O
A T G A R A G E □ O T
N O Y N O U R R □ C A
□ □ P R I Z E E P K R
N ● E J U D H V A A E
E I D □ S T I O R T G
E M L L E B □ L T T I
R S A S A C K V S H R
C T O R S A N I O E F
S L N A F R O N T □ E
C □ □ A B □ B G L E R
F O L D I N G □ W A Y
```

136. SEEDING THE CLOUDS

Shaped like a rain cloud with a bolt of lightning, the grid contains words that can all be created by rearranging the letters in RAIN CLOUDS. Every word contains from 4 to 9 letters (from the 10 different letters in RAIN CLOUDS) and no letter is ever repeated. All the words in the hidden message also come from the letters in RAIN CLOUDS, and the message tells you how movie star/governor Schwarzenegger may have once made money in Egypt's capital. (When you're done with the puzzle, try another game and see how many more words you can find from the letters in RAIN CLOUDS.)

ACORN		
AIRS	CASINO	CORAL
ALOUD	CAULDRONS	COUSIN
AROUND	CLAN	DINOSAUR
AUDIO	COAL	DRAIN

```
      C  O  U  S  I  N        A  I  R  S
   A  A  R  O  U  N  D  I  N  O  S  A  U  R
R  N  U  N  O  N  S  A  L  I  D  A  D  N  S  O
R  O  L  I  A  S  L  U  C  S  S  U  I  D  A  R
A  L  D  A  D  O  C  A  R  L  O  D  O  I
   C  R  R  U  C  S  L  C  A  I  I  R  A  C
   O  D  A  I  S  O  U  N  C  O  I  L  I
   N  N  R  N  A  A  O  L  D  N  I  A  D
   S  O  N  L  A  R  O  C  C  N
                     L
                  A
               D  N  I  R
                  A
                  L
               O
            S  A  I
               R
            O
```

ICARUS	RADIO	SOLAR
IRONCLAD	RADIUS	SUNDIAL
ISLAND	RIND	UNCOIL
OILCANS	SAILOR	UNSOCIAL

137. HAPPY ENDING

Shaped like a magic wand, the grid contains things you might wish for. The hidden message tells you what you might do to get your wishes.

BEAUTY

COURAGE

FAME

FOOD

HEALTH

HELP

LOVE

MONEY

PEACE

POWER

PUPPY

[YOUR OWN] ROOM

SLEEP

SNOW DAY

STRAIGHT A'S

[TO BE] TALL

```
            W
            R
      I  E  S
      H  M  W  F  Y
U  H  L  L  A  T  O  H  T  L  A  E  H
   P  E  F  E  O  P  P  U  P  P  Y
      L  D  G  Y  E  A  O
      P  E  A  C  E
      N  N  L  D  R  B  L
   R  O  O  M  W  A  U  S  S
   M  V  T     O     A  O  R
   E           N           C
               S
               T
               R
               A
               I
               G
               H
               T
               A
               S
```

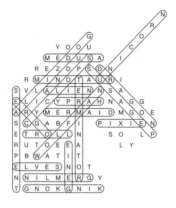

1.
THAT'S FANTASTIC!

"You're driving me absolutely batty!"

2.
BE A GOOD SPORT

Because she's a rock 'n' rollerblader.

3.
WHIRLED VIEW

World-famous.

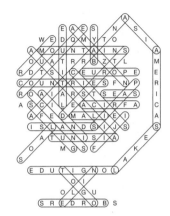

4.
UP A TREE

He took chemis-tree and geome-tree.

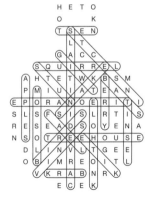

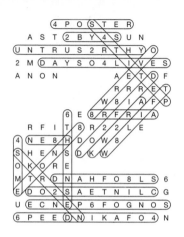

5.

2, 4, 6, 8

A stuntwoman on a freighter fired her six-gun.

6.

POOL PARTY

He knew it was either sink or swim.

7.
CAN YOU STAND IT?

It's a bandstand handstand.

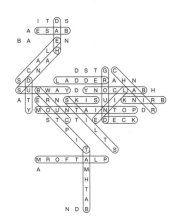

8.
MY I

Zuchini, calamari, and souvlaki.

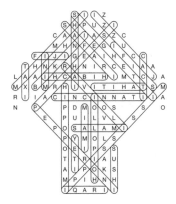

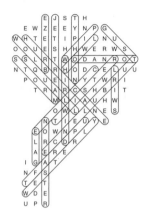

9.
BLOWHARDS

She went into her windup with the wind up.

10.
TEAM PLAYERS

Bengal, Colt, Falcon, Jaguar, Jet, Ram.

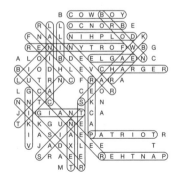

11.
PLAY GROUND

A person who's making a snow angel.

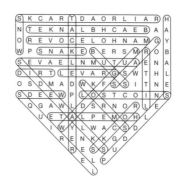

12.
THE SOUND OF MUSIC

She put it in her "note" book.

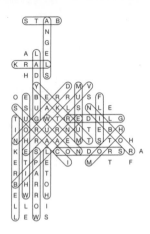

13.
WINGING IT

"...a horse that flies?"

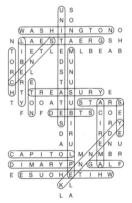

14.
IT'S ONLY
MONEY

"Soon she'll be able to afford an umbrella."

15.
IN A FIX

We give great self-service.

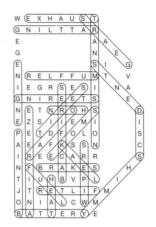

16.
AW, CHUTE!

"...don't take up parachuting."

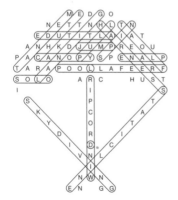

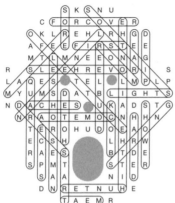

17.
OFF WITH HER HEAD!

Knuckle, hammer, sleepy, and thunder.

18.
JUMP FOR JOY

Playing a game can make you feel kind of jumpy.

19.
A TALL TALE

It's the Giants.

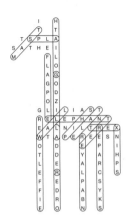

20.
THAT'S NEWS TO ME!

"...except that they happened to different people."

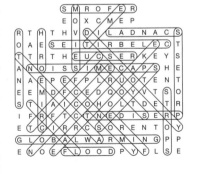

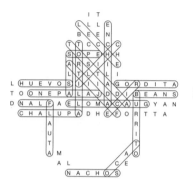

21.
HOT STUFF
It'll be chili today and
hot tamale.

22.
CLEAN UP
YOUR ACT
They wanted to make a
clean getaway.

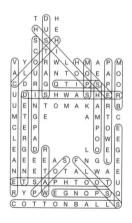

23.
FOWL PLAY

"...they were for
the birds."

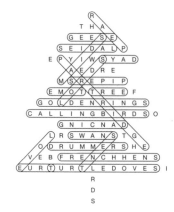

24.
HOW SWEET
IT IS

"...so now I have it as
an appetizer."

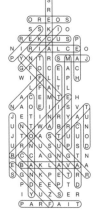

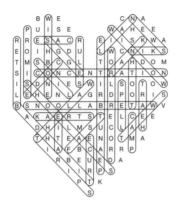

25.
TAKE A BREAK

Because he said,
"Come on. Give me
a break!"

26.
TOOLING ALONG

"...held up a hammer
and saw."

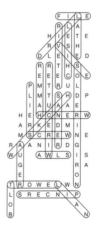

27.
HURRY UP AND GET DOWN TO BUSINESS

"Sit down and shut up!"

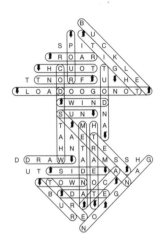

28.
ROLL CALL

They wanted to be "roll models."

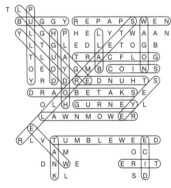

29.
STRIP
SEARCH

Garfield and Mallard Fillmore. [James A. Garfield and Millard Fillmore]

30.
GOING PLACES

In Monopoly, the only "place" to go is Park Place.

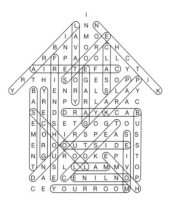

31.
SHAKE ON IT

Holding a snow globe can make you feel really shaky.

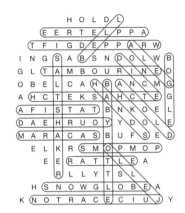

32.
THAT'S STRETCHING IT

"It's the seventh-inning stretch."

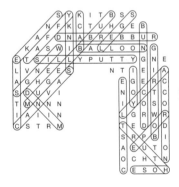

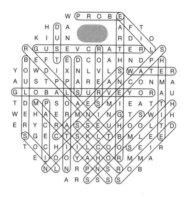

33.
MISSION TO MARS

What kind of candy
will astronauts eat
when they get here?

Mars Bars.

34.
JUST SAY
NO

Ge<u>no</u>a is <u>not</u> <u>n</u>orth of
<u>Nor</u>way.

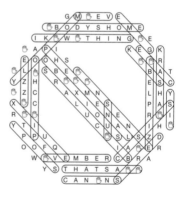

35.
TAKING IT ALL IN

Responsibility.

36.
HOLD ON!

A new world record.

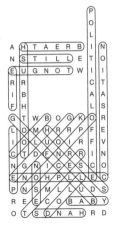

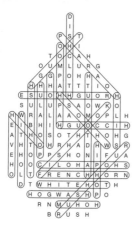

37.
WATERLOGGED

I thought I saw a photograph of a thornbush.

38.
PAY ATTENTION!

"C'mon now, knock it off!"

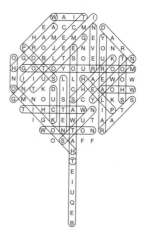

39.
KNOCK IT OFF!

Tossing and turning.

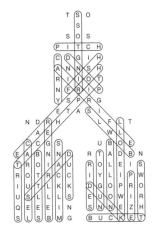

40.
WHAT SMELLS?

Fish market, fresh laundry, and bad breath.

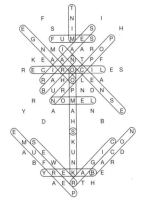

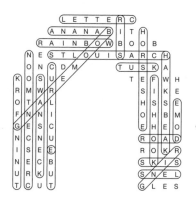

41.
MARKING ON THE CURVE

"...to bend the rules."

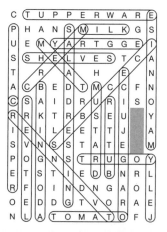

42.
OPEN THE DOOR!

Change the first letter in "good" to an F.

43.
SEA HERE!

"...lose a bet on Seabiscuit"

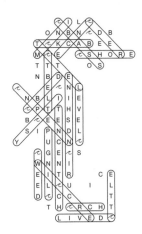

44.
ZIP IT UP

"...zip right to follow a
Zip Code?"

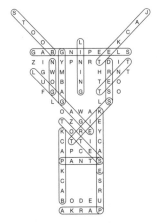

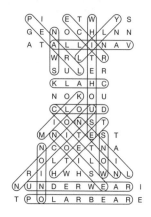

45.
GET IT WHITE

"It's gonna turn out all white."

46.
A THIRST FOR WORDS

A boxer's favorite drink is punch.

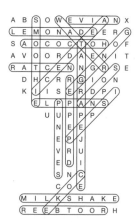

47.
Y NOT?

Yabba-dabba-doo!

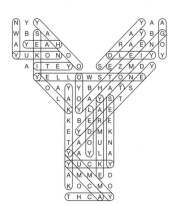

48.
PUT ON A HAPPY FACE

I doubt the saying "happy as a clam" applies to a clam in chowder.

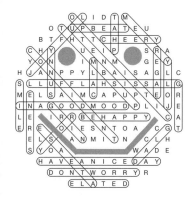

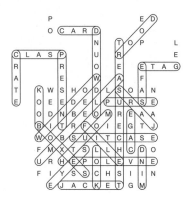

49.
OPEN FOR BUSINESS

People who need bait for fishing.

50.
WHAT AN ICE GAME

The goalie didn't wear a face mask. [It hadn't been invented.]

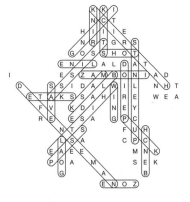

306

51.
PLUG IT IN

He took a big gulp instead. [GULP = PLUG backwards.]

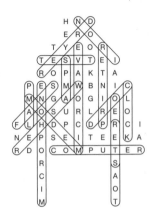

52.
I NEED THIS RIDE NOW!

A roller coaster.

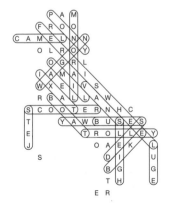

53.
NEW YORK, NEW YORK

"...it's commonly called 'the city that never sleeps.'"

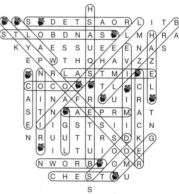

54.
AW, NUTS!

"...it makes sense that 'nut' is in nutritious."

55.
LOSER!

He lost interest.

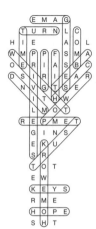

56.
GET A LOAD OF THIS!

Porsche.

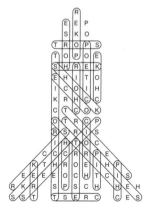

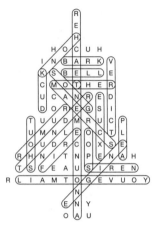

57.
LISTEN UP

"Huh? I couldn't hear you."

58.
ON THE GO

You might go directly to Go.

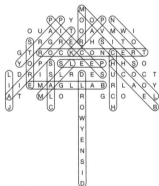

59.
SOFT IN THE HEAD

President Teddy Roosevelt.

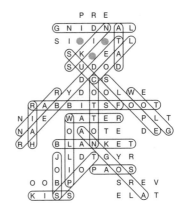

60.
FLOATING AWAY

"...to have a root beer float."

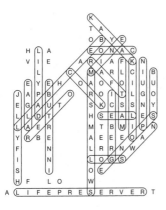

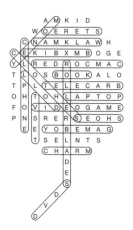

61.
IT'S A GIFT!

A kid who gets a lot of presents.

62.
PUT YOUR HOUSE IN ORDER

A housebroken dog broke into a house.

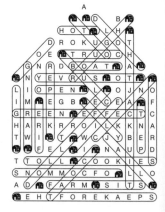

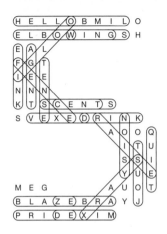

63.
TAKE FIVE

"Oh, some G-U-Y."
[G, U, and Y are the
missing initial letters in
the word list.]

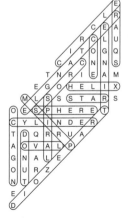

64.
GET INTO
SHAPE

Times Square.

65.
IT LOOKS LIKE REIGN

Each is a ruler.

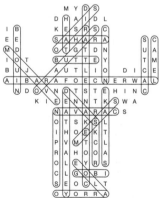

66.
JUST DESERTS

"My dad liked it, but I didn't think it was so hot."

67.
CLOWNING AROUND

Dandelion tamer.

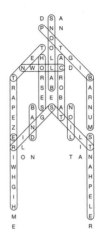

68.
IT ALL ADDS UP

"Can I give you sum help?"

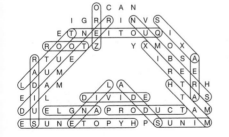

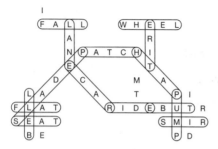

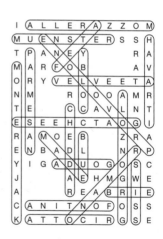

71.
I'D LIKE TO POINT OUT...

She said, "Did you get my point?"

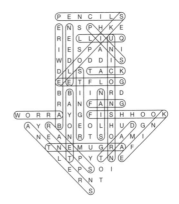

72.
SOMETHING IS FISHY

Peanut butter and jellyfish.

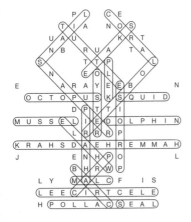

317

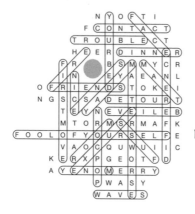

73.
MAKING DECISIONS

Not if they're looking to make a quick getaway.

74.
IT'S A PUT-ON

"Play a French horn but not a shoehorn."

318

75.
TOTAL ECLIPSE OF THE MOON

...base of a fingernail.

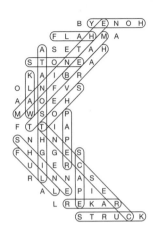

76.
GREENHOUSE

[The] Incredible Hulk, Kermit the Frog, and [the] Grinch.

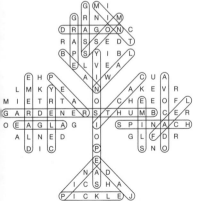

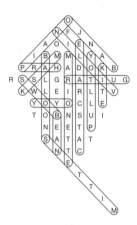

77.
STRINGS ATTACHED

"Forget it!"

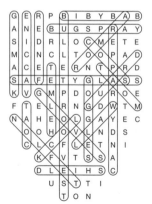

78.
PLAYING IT SAFE

Protect and defend the Constitution.

79.
ARE YOU PACKED?

Try to pack as much in as you can.

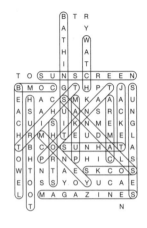

80.
I STRAIN

I think it stinks.

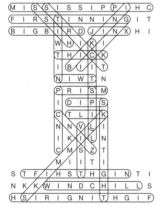

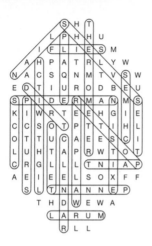

81.
WALL-DONE

Humpty wasn't weird,
but he was off-the-wall.

82.
HOW DOES YOUR GARDEN GROW?

"If you carrot all, please lettuce in."

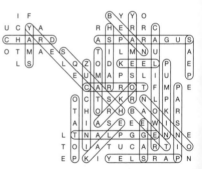

83.
BACK TO THE DRAWING BOARD

Because she was quick on the draw.

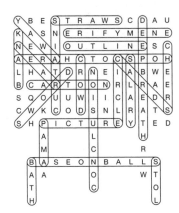

84.
PANDEMONIUM

Spanish omelets and some marzipan.

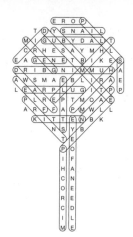

85.
ALL SMALL

They make small talk.

86.
GET THE MESSAGE?

UISFF NBZ LFFQ B
TFDSFU JG UXP BSF
EFBE, which becomes
"Three may keep a secret
if two [of them] are dead."

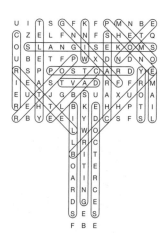

87.
FLAG DAY

He'd be the star-spangled
Bruce Banner.

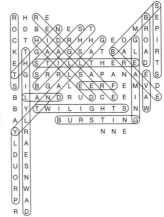

88.
NOW WE'RE COOKING!

"...but in a blender I get
all mixed up."

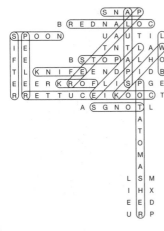

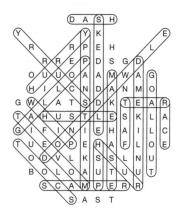

89.
QUICKLY!

He's going at
full blast.

90.
TAKE A PEAK

"Don't worry. I'm right
on his trail."

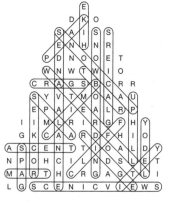

91.
MAKING A CHANGE

One to hold the bulb, and one to rotate the ladder.

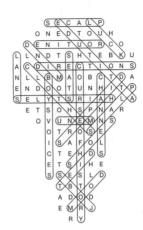

92.
WIN-WIN SITUATION

"...but wanting to win is."

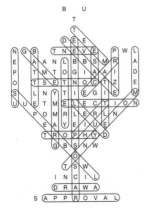

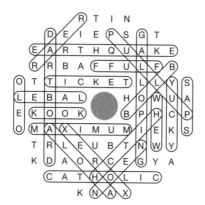

93.
START AT THE END

Tiniest bathtub kayak.

94.
LET'S CALL IT A DAY

"And don't forget to brush your teeth!"

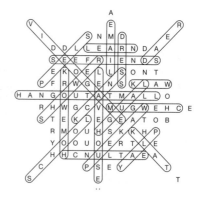

95.
IT'S A START

"Let's get off to a flying start!"

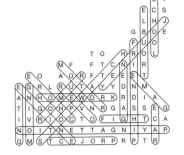

96.
Ant-icipation

The elephant had ants in his pants.

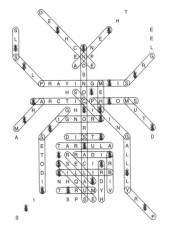

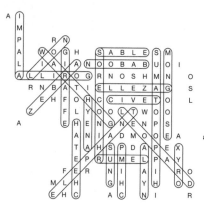

97.
OUT OF AFRICA

A rhino's horn is hollow and made from hair.

98.
AMERICA'S FAVORITE PASTA- TIME

She said, "I think you're full of bologna."

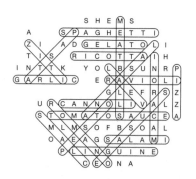

99.
WHAT AN ICE IDEA

They said she was a cheapskate.

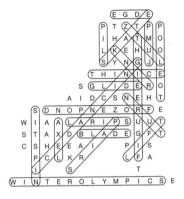

100.
HANG IN THERE

"I can't seem to get the hang of it."

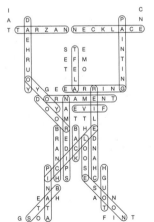

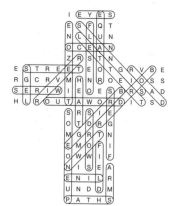

101.
CROSS-
EXAMINATION

It never crossed
his mind.

102.
START AT
THE END
...AGAIN

Roger sips pop and
says it's yummy.

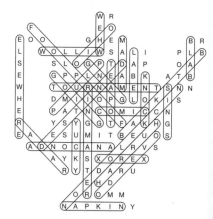

332

103.
IT'S IN THE CARDS

It's the on deck circle.

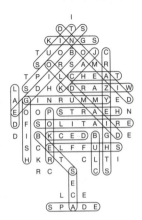

104.
TRAINING SESSION

She said, "You've got a one-track mind."

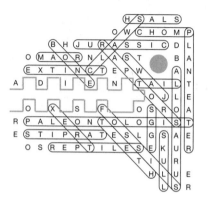

105.
LOOKING FOR FOSSILS

"Oh, don't be a dino-sore loser!"

106.
QUEUING UP

A squid squeezed into a square aquarium.

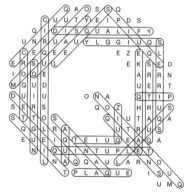

107.
MELLOW YELLOW

Big Bird and Tweety and Pikachu.

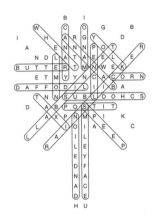

108.
PLAYING IN THE PARK

They're nuts about nuts.

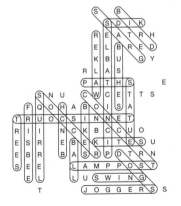

109.
TUTTI-FRUITY
They are not inside but
on the outside.

110.
DESK
JOCKY

You get a rubber-Band-
Aid. [rubber band +
Band-Aid]

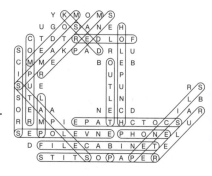

111.
HATS ENTERTAINMENT

"That's enough of that!"
"That's what you think!"

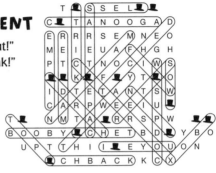

112.
CAPITOL LETTERS

Macaws, a raccoon, and even a dairy cow. [A century apart, the macaws belonged to Dolley Madison and Teddy Roosevelt; the raccoon to Mrs. Coolidge; and a dairy cow named Pauline to President Taft.]

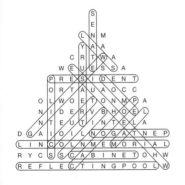

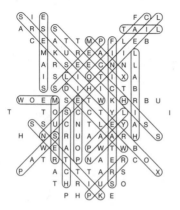

113.
CAT-22

If a cat burns its butt,
is that a catastrophe?

114.
RUN
FOR IT!

His nose runs and
his feet smell.

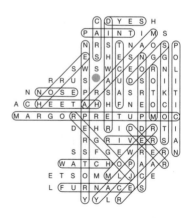

338

115.
POLICE
SEARCH

"Always say police
and thank you."

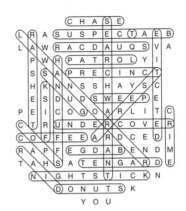

116.
CHOCK FULL OF
CHOCOLATE

"...to eat a whole lot
more chocolate."

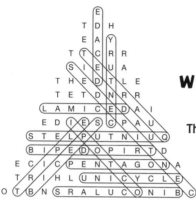

117.
WHAT'S YOUR NUMBER?

The <u>triathlete</u> tried a <u>decathlon</u>.

118.
PLAYTIME

Shortstop and piano.

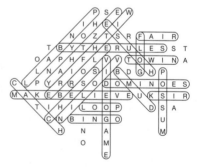

119.
THE RULING CLASS

Thin<u>king</u> and blin<u>king</u>.

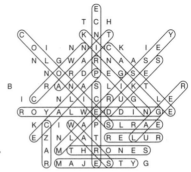

120.
CATCHING COLD

"I hate winter!" said Tom coldly.

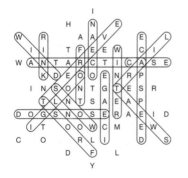

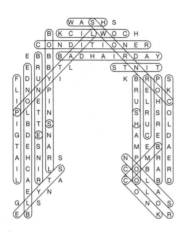

121.
HAIRPIECES

She likes bangs.

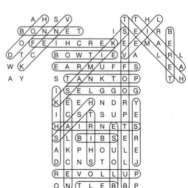

122.
TO TOP IT ALL OFF

"...a shirt always ends up on top."

123.
YOU'RE ASKING FOR IT!

In-formation
information.

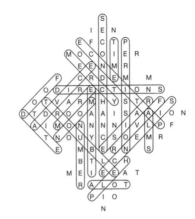

124.
NAME-DROPPING

Paki<u>stan</u>, Den<u>mark</u>.

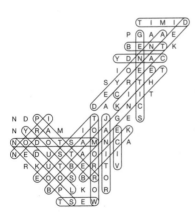

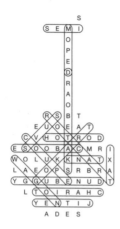

125.
THE WHEEL DEAL

Steamrollerblades.
[steamroller + Rollerblades]

126.
FILL IN THE WORDS

That would be Phil R. Rupp [which sounds like "Fill 'er up!"].

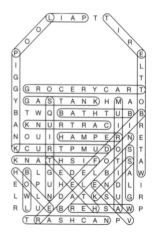

127.
COLOR I.D.

In living color.

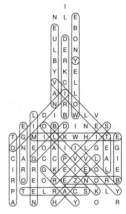

128.
BOO CAREFUL!

They're giving out Halloweenies.

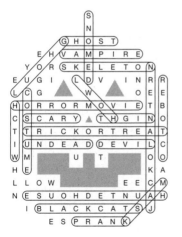

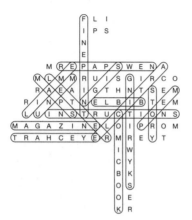

129.
READ ALL ABOUT IT

Lips, music, or a thermometer.

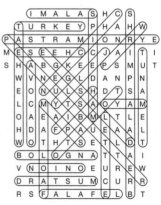

130.
SLICE OF LIFE

"Ham is best, and the liverwurst [worst]."

131.
SHELL GAME

William Tell.

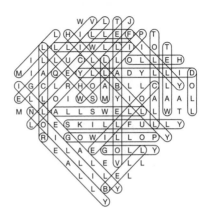

132.
PACKING A PUNCH

Because each of them is a knockout.

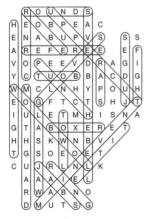

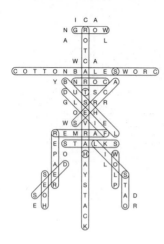

133.
FIELD DAY

"I can always grow older."

134.
WHAT'S THE QUESTION?

To show he wasn't chicken.

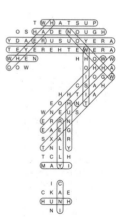

348

135.
KNOCK KNOCK

"I think you're just so a-door-able!"

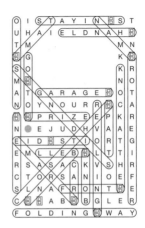

136.
SEEDING THE CLOUDS

Arnold sold colas in old Cairo.

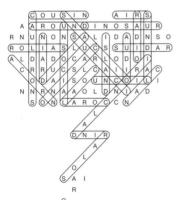

137.
HAPPY
ENDING

Wish upon a star.

PUZZLE 117: WHAT'S YOUR NUMBER?

PREFIX MEANINGS

BI- means "two"

CENT- (one hundred)

DEC- (ten)

OCTO- (eight)

PENTA- (five)

QUART- (four)

QUINT- (five)

TRI- (three)

UNI- (one)

PUZZLE 124: NAME DROPPING

NAMES

ANNoyed	JANitor	thingamaBOB
BENt	KITe	TIMid
bRICK	LOUd	tisSUE
cANDY	mastoDON	TOMorrow
creaTED	PATter	VICe
GENEtics	spoKEN	WESt
iRON	STUdy	

About the Author

Mark Danna is a longtime and full-time puzzlemaker who has created more picture-shaped word searches than anyone else. Besides his fifteen-plus books for Sterling, Danna writes the syndicated newspaper puzzle Wordy Gurdy, a page-a-day puzzle calendar for Mensa, crosswords for *The New York Times*, and a variety of puzzles for various clients. Danna learned his craft under the tutelage of NPR puzzlemaster Will Shortz during a seven-year stint at *Games* magazine. Danna has also been a staff writer for a prime time TV game show and a daily trivia quiz writer for CNN.com. Prior to puzzling, Danna won three national Frisbee titles and wrote a how-to book that was round and came packaged inside a Frisbee.